Exploring the Cosmos

EXPLORING THE COSMOS

First edition. March 19, 2025.

Copyright © 2025 Milano.

ISBN: 979-8227645494

Written by Milano.

Dedication

To all the dreamers, both young and old, who gaze at the night sky and wonder—this book is dedicated to you. Your curiosity fuels the exploration that unfolds within these pages, a testament to the enduring human spirit of inquiry and our unwavering thirst for knowledge. This work is also dedicated to the countless scientists, engineers, and researchers whose dedication and tireless efforts have made the exploration and understanding of the cosmos possible.

Their contributions, from the earliest astronomical observations to the latest technological advancements, continue to pave the way for a deeper understanding of our place in the universe. Finally, this book is dedicated to those unsung heroes, the individuals who support the dreams of others, providing the encouragement and resources necessary to reach for the stars. Their unwavering belief in the potential of human ingenuity is the bedrock upon which scientific progress is built.

Preface

The cosmos, that boundless expanse of stars, galaxies, and mysteries, has captivated humankind for millennia. From ancient stargazers charting the movements of celestial bodies to modern scientists unraveling the universe's deepest secrets, our fascination with space remains undimmed. This book aims to share that wonder, to translate the complex language of astrophysics into a narrative accessible to all. "Exploring the Cosmos" is not just a textbook; it's an invitation to journey through the universe, to witness the grandeur of nebulae, the power of quasars, and the delicate dance of planets around distant suns. We'll delve into the intricacies of planetary formation, explore the possibility of extraterrestrial life, and grapple with the mind-bending concepts of dark matter and dark energy. This exploration is not limited to the grand scale; we will also focus on the details, on the exquisite beauty of celestial phenomena revealed by modern telescopes and instruments. We will look at the methods and technologies that allow us to peer into this vastness, from radio waves to gamma rays, and examine how the combination of these different wavelengths paints a complete picture of the cosmos. Whether you're a seasoned astronomer or a curious beginner, I hope this book ignites your own passion for exploration, fostering a deeper appreciation for the extraordinary universe in which we reside. Prepare for a journey that will expand your understanding of the cosmos and leave you with a profound sense of awe and wonder. This book is a testament to the fact that exploration of the universe is ongoing and that new discoveries and technologies continually expand our knowledge base. The more we learn, the more questions arise, driving us to further explore the great unknown.

Introduction

Our journey into the cosmos begins with a simple yet profound question: What is the universe? This seemingly straightforward query opens the door to a realm of unimaginable scale, complexity, and wonder. For centuries, humanity has gazed at the night sky, pondering the nature of the stars, the planets, and the vast expanse that stretches beyond our own pale blue dot. From ancient myths to modern scientific theories, the quest to understand the universe has shaped our cultures, our technologies, and our very understanding of ourselves. In this book, we embark on an exploration of the universe, combining scientific accuracy with engaging narrative to paint a vivid picture of the cosmos. Our journey will take us from the familiar landscape of our own planet to the far reaches of space, revealing the wonders and mysteries that lie within. We will examine the birth and death of stars, the formation of galaxies, and the dance of planets around distant suns. We will explore the search for extraterrestrial life, ponder the nature of dark matter and dark energy, and contemplate the universe's ultimate fate. We'll navigate the electromagnetic spectrum, exploring how different wavelengths reveal different aspects of celestial bodies, from the cool dust of a planetary nebula to the scorching plasma of a star's corona. But this is more than a simple recitation of facts. We will consider the historical context of astronomical discoveries, the innovative technologies that have made those discoveries possible, and the ongoing scientific inquiries that continue to push the boundaries of our knowledge. Prepare for a captivating exploration of the universe, a journey that combines scientific rigor with the sheer wonder of discovery, reminding us of our place in this vast and magnificent cosmos.

Understanding the Scale of the Universe

Our journey into the cosmos begins with a fundamental yet awe-inspiring concept: scale. The universe is unimaginably vast, dwarfing even our most ambitious imaginings. To comprehend its enormity, we need to develop a sense of cosmic proportion, a skill honed by centuries of astronomical observation and theoretical breakthroughs. Let's start by addressing the units of measurement we use to navigate this incredible expanse.

The familiar kilometer or even the mile, while useful for terrestrial travel, are utterly inadequate when charting the distances between stars and galaxies. Instead, astronomers employ units reflecting the colossal distances involved: the light-year and the parsec. A light-year, as its name suggests, is the distance light travels in a single year. Given the speed of light – approximately 300,000 kilometers per second – a light-year equates to roughly 9.46 trillion kilometers. It's a number so large it's almost impossible to fully grasp.

Imagine trying to drive that distance in a car; the journey would far outlast any conceivable human lifespan.

To further illustrate this, consider our nearest stellar neighbor, Proxima Centauri. This red dwarf star is located approximately 4.24 light-years from our Sun. That means it takes light, the fastest thing in the universe, over four years to travel from Proxima Centauri to Earth. Any information we receive from this star is, therefore, over four years old. We're essentially looking into the past when we observe it.

The parsec, another unit frequently used in astronomy, is roughly 3.26 light-years. While seemingly just another unit, the parsec's origin is tied to a clever trigonometric calculation involving parallax, a shift in the apparent position of a nearby star against the background of more distant stars as observed from Earth at different points in its orbit around the Sun. This subtle shift allows astronomers to triangulate the distance to nearby stars, ultimately leading to the definition of the parsec.

Now, let's use these units to explore the scale of our solar system. The distance from the Sun to Earth, known as one astronomical unit (AU), is about 150 million kilometers.

While considerable, this pales in comparison to the distances between stars. The outer reaches of our solar system, defined by the heliopause – the boundary where the Sun's influence gives way to interstellar space – extends to roughly 100 AU. Even this considerable distance is a mere speck compared to the scale of our galaxy.

Our solar system, with its eight planets, countless asteroids, comets, and dwarf planets, resides within the Milky Way Galaxy, a colossal spiral galaxy containing hundreds of billions of stars. The diameter of the Milky Way is estimated to be around 100,000 light-years. To truly grasp this number, imagine traveling at the speed of light; it would take you 100,000 years to traverse the galaxy from one end to the other. Think of it: the light we see from the farthest reaches of our galaxy today left those stars 100,000 years ago, a time long before human civilization existed.

But the Milky Way, impressive as it is, is just one galaxy among billions, perhaps trillions, in the observable universe. The observable universe refers to the portion of the cosmos we can currently see, limited by the finite speed of light and the age of the universe. The size of the observable universe is estimated to be around 93 billion light-years in diameter. It's a number that defies easy comprehension.

Early astronomers, lacking the sophisticated tools we possess today, made remarkable strides in understanding cosmic scales. The ancient Greeks, for example, attempted to measure the size of the Earth and the distance to the Moon and Sun, albeit with limited accuracy by today's standards.

Their efforts, however, laid the foundation for future generations of astronomers who, with the invention of the telescope, made increasingly precise measurements and discoveries. Figures like Tycho Brahe, with his meticulous observations of planetary positions, and Johannes Kepler, with his laws of planetary motion, significantly advanced our understanding of celestial distances.

The advent of modern techniques, such as parallax measurements, spectroscopic analysis (studying the light emitted by stars), and the use of standard candles (objects of known luminosity), have revolutionized our ability to measure cosmic distances. Standard candles, such as Cepheid variable stars and Type Ia supernovae, allow astronomers to measure distances to faraway galaxies with remarkable accuracy. These methods have helped to map the distribution of galaxies in the universe and refine our understanding of its vastness.

The sheer scale of the universe leads us to confront the humbling realization of our relatively minuscule place within it. Our planet, our solar system, even our galaxy, represent but a tiny fraction of the cosmos's entirety. Yet, it's within this seemingly insignificant corner that we, as humans, have developed the capacity to comprehend, to some degree, the awe-inspiring immensity that surrounds us. The journey to grasp these scales isn't merely an intellectual exercise; it's a transformative experience that redefines our relationship with the universe and our place within it. And this understanding, this newfound perspective, is what fuels our continued exploration and desire to unravel the mysteries of the cosmos.

Let's not forget the human element in this vast cosmic narrative. The quest to understand the scale of the universe has been a driving force behind scientific innovation for centuries. Each new measurement, each refinement of our understanding, has led to a deeper appreciation of the universe's complexity and magnificence. This relentless pursuit of knowledge, this insatiable curiosity, is a testament to the human spirit and our unwavering desire to comprehend the world around us. It's a journey that continues to this day, with new discoveries constantly reshaping our understanding of cosmic distances and the universe's vast expanse.

To visualize the staggering distances, consider this thought experiment: If we were to shrink the Sun down to the size of a grapefruit, Earth would be the size of a pinhead, approximately 15 meters away. Jupiter, a giant in our solar system, would be about the size of a small marble, some 75 meters from the grapefruit Sun. Now, imagine the nearest star, Proxima Centauri, at this scale. It would be located thousands of kilometers away – roughly the distance between New York City and London. This simple analogy, though imperfect, offers a tangible representation of the sheer scale separating even our closest stellar neighbors.

Extending this further to encompass the Milky Way Galaxy, we would find ourselves in a scenario where our grapefruit Sun would be among trillions of other pinheads, peppered across an area spanning millions of kilometers. And then, to truly grasp the scale of the observable universe, we'd need to contemplate an area many orders of magnitude larger than this, an immensity that stretches our imagination beyond its limits. Yet, this staggering vastness is what makes the exploration of the cosmos so compelling and endlessly fascinating. The journey into the depths of space is not just a journey into the physical, but a journey into the profound mysteries of the universe and our place within it, a journey that continues to unfold before our eyes, fueled by scientific discovery and human curiosity.

The Electromagnetic Spectrum and its Significance

Our journey to understand the cosmos' vastness continues with a closer look at the information carrier that allows us to observe the universe: electromagnetic radiation. This isn't just the light we see; it's a much broader spectrum encompassing a range of wavelengths, each carrying unique information about the celestial objects that emit them. This electromagnetic spectrum is the key that unlocks the universe's secrets, revealing details invisible to the naked eye.

The electromagnetic spectrum is a continuous distribution of electromagnetic waves, arranged according to their frequency or wavelength. At one end lies radio waves, with the longest wavelengths and lowest frequencies, stretching out to kilometers in length. Then come microwaves, used in everyday appliances but also crucial in astronomical observations. Moving further along the spectrum, we encounter infrared radiation, often associated with heat. This is followed by visible light, the narrow band of radiation our eyes can detect, encompassing the familiar colors of the rainbow – red, orange, yellow, green, blue, indigo, and violet. Beyond visible light lies ultraviolet radiation, responsible for sunburns and invisible to our eyes but crucial for many biological processes and studied extensively by astronomers. Next are X-rays, highly energetic radiation used in medical imaging and capable of penetrating dense materials, offering unique insights into high-energy celestial phenomena. Finally, at the high-frequency end of the spectrum, are gamma rays, the most energetic form of electromagnetic radiation, born from extreme cosmic events such as supernovae and active galactic nuclei.

Each type of electromagnetic radiation interacts with matter differently. Radio waves can penetrate dust clouds that obscure visible light, allowing astronomers to study regions of space otherwise hidden. Microwaves are useful for studying the cosmic microwave background radiation, the afterglow of the Big Bang. Infrared radiation can penetrate dust clouds as well, revealing the formation of stars within them, and also allows the study of cooler objects like planets. Visible light allows us to see the universe as we commonly perceive it, revealing the colors and brightness of stars and galaxies. Ultraviolet radiation provides information about the temperature and composition of stars, as well as revealing the presence of hot gas in nebulae. X-rays reveal the high-energy processes in the universe, such as black holes and neutron stars, illuminating the hot, dense regions surrounding these objects. Gamma rays are a direct indicator of the most violent events in the cosmos, providing a glimpse into phenomena like supernova explosions and gamma-ray bursts.

The ability to detect and analyze the entire electromagnetic spectrum is paramount to modern astronomy. Different parts of the spectrum provide complementary information, revealing a more comprehensive picture of celestial objects than any single wavelength alone could offer. This is why astronomers utilize a diverse array of telescopes, each specifically designed to detect a particular range of wavelengths. Radio telescopes, often large dish-shaped antennas, collect radio waves emitted by celestial objects.

Microwave telescopes operate similarly and are vital for cosmic microwave background studies. Infrared telescopes are designed to detect infrared radiation, often equipped with specialized cooling systems to minimize interference from the telescope's own heat. Optical telescopes, familiar to most, are designed to detect visible light. Ultraviolet, X-ray, and gamma-ray telescopes are more complex, often requiring instruments launched into space to avoid atmospheric absorption of these high-energy wavelengths.

The use of different wavelengths has led to groundbreaking discoveries in astronomy. Radio astronomy, for instance, has revealed the existence of pulsars, rapidly rotating neutron stars that emit beams of radio waves. Microwaves have allowed the confirmation of the Big Bang theory through the detection of the cosmic microwave background radiation.

Infrared astronomy has helped us study the birthplaces of stars, revealing the processes of star formation hidden within dust clouds. Optical astronomy continues to reveal the structure and evolution of galaxies, allowing us to classify them and map their distributions. Ultraviolet astronomy has provided information about the composition and temperatures of stars and their atmospheres. X-ray astronomy has unveiled active galactic nuclei, powered by supermassive black holes, and has revealed the existence of powerful X-ray emitting binary stars. Finally, gamma-ray astronomy has provided insights into the most energetic phenomena in the universe, such as gamma-ray bursts, which are among the most luminous events ever observed.

Consider the example of a supernova remnant, the expanding cloud of gas and dust left behind after a massive star explodes. By observing this remnant across the electromagnetic spectrum, we gain a vastly richer understanding of the event. Optical observations might reveal the remnant's overall shape and brightness. Infrared observations could reveal the temperature and composition of the dust and gas within the remnant. X-ray observations would show the hot, shocked gas, revealing the details of the explosion's dynamics and the remnant's interaction with the surrounding interstellar medium. Radio observations might show the emission from highly energetic electrons accelerated by the shockwave, revealing the remnant's magnetic field structure. Each wavelength reveals a different aspect, and by combining the data, astronomers create a highly detailed 3D model of the supernova's evolution.

The electromagnetic spectrum is not simply a tool for observation; it's a fundamental element of our understanding of the universe's physical laws and processes. It provides a window into the physical conditions of celestial objects— their temperature, density, chemical composition, and magnetic fields. The spectrum allows us to analyze the motion of objects through redshift and blueshift, to measure distances and understand the universe's expansion. The study of spectral lines, specific wavelengths absorbed or emitted by atoms and molecules, tells us about the composition of stars and planets and reveals the presence of specific elements.

Further, the electromagnetic spectrum allows us to study the universe across vast stretches of time. The light we see from distant galaxies has traveled for billions of years, providing us with a glimpse into the early universe. By analyzing the properties of this light, we can understand how the universe has evolved, learning about the conditions that existed billions of years ago. The ongoing exploration of the electromagnetic spectrum remains one of the most dynamic and exciting fields of astronomy, continuously refining our knowledge of the universe and its evolution. It's a testament to the power of scientific inquiry, continuously revealing new secrets about the cosmos and expanding our understanding of our place within this vast and mysterious universe.

The power of combining observations from different parts of the spectrum is particularly relevant when studying the early universe. The cosmic microwave background radiation, a relic from the Big Bang, is primarily detected in the microwave portion of the spectrum. However, the subtle temperature fluctuations within the CMB, which provide crucial information about the early universe's structure and composition, require high-precision measurements across a broad range of frequencies. Similarly, the study of the formation of the first galaxies requires observations across multiple wavelengths. The initial collapse of gas clouds, which predates the formation of stars, is best detected in the infrared and radio portions of the spectrum. The subsequent star formation within these galaxies is revealed through optical and ultraviolet observations, while the high-energy processes in the galaxies are highlighted by X-ray and gamma-ray observations.

As technology advances, our ability to explore the electromagnetic spectrum expands, enabling increasingly refined observations and a deeper understanding of the universe. New instruments are continuously being developed, pushing the boundaries of detection sensitivity and spectral resolution. This allows astronomers to probe fainter sources, uncover more subtle details, and extend our reach deeper into space and time. The ongoing evolution of telescope technology, both ground-based and space-based, is crucial for continued progress in unraveling the universe's mysteries. The future of astronomy lies in these continuing advances, driving us further toward a comprehensive understanding of the cosmos and our place within it.

Basic Celestial Mechanics Orbits and Gravity

Our understanding of the universe's vastness and the information it reveals through electromagnetic radiation lays the foundation for exploring another crucial aspect of space science: celestial mechanics. This field delves into the fundamental principles governing the movement of celestial bodies, primarily driven by the force of gravity.

Understanding gravity's influence is paramount to comprehending the structure and evolution of our solar system, galaxies, and the universe itself.

At the heart of celestial mechanics lies Newton's Law of Universal Gravitation. This elegantly simple law states that every particle in the universe attracts every other particle with a force directly proportional to the product of their masses and inversely proportional to the square of the distance between their centers. In simpler terms, the more massive the objects, the stronger the gravitational pull between them; and the farther apart they are, the weaker the pull becomes. This inverse-square relationship is key to understanding why planets move the way they do.

Imagine a lone star, massive and radiating energy. Now, picture a smaller object, perhaps a planet, nearby. The star's immense gravity exerts a powerful force on the planet, constantly pulling it inward. However, the planet isn't simply falling into the star. It also possesses its own momentum, an initial velocity that could be attributed to the initial conditions of its formation, or the effects of collisions and interactions within the early solar system. This velocity gives the planet a tendency to move in a straight line, tangential to its orbit around the star.

The interplay between the inward pull of gravity and the planet's tangential velocity results in a curved path – an orbit. The planet continuously falls toward the star, but its sideways motion prevents it from ever actually hitting the star. The balance between these two forces is what keeps the planet in its orbit, resulting in the stable trajectories we observe in our solar system and beyond.

The shape of a planet's orbit is not always a perfect circle. Most planetary orbits are elliptical, meaning they are oval- shaped. This is a direct consequence of the interplay between gravity and initial velocity. A perfectly circular orbit would require an incredibly precise balance between the two, a condition rarely achieved in the chaotic environment of a forming solar system. The eccentricity of an ellipse describes how elongated it is, ranging from 0 (a perfect circle) to 1 (a parabola, where the object is not gravitationally bound and escapes).

Within an elliptical orbit, there are two key points to consider: the perihelion and the aphelion. The perihelion is the point in a planet's orbit where it is closest to the star; conversely, the aphelion is the point where it is farthest. A planet's speed is not constant throughout its orbit. Due to the inverse square law, gravitational force is stronger at perihelion, causing the planet to accelerate. As it moves away from the star towards aphelion, the gravitational force weakens, causing the planet to decelerate. This constant change in speed throughout its orbit is a critical element of understanding planetary motion.

Kepler's Laws of Planetary Motion provide a more precise mathematical description of these orbital characteristics.

Kepler's First Law states that the orbit of each planet is an ellipse with the Sun at one focus. Kepler's Second Law, the Law of Equal Areas, states that a line joining a planet and the Sun sweeps out equal areas during equal intervals of time. This means that a planet moves faster when it's closer to the Sun (perihelion) and slower when it's farther away (aphelion). Finally, Kepler's Third Law, the Law of Harmonies, states that the square of the orbital period of a planet is directly proportional to the cube of the semi-major axis of its orbit. The semi-major axis is essentially the average distance of the planet from the Sun. This law allows us to relate the orbital period of a planet to its average distance from the star.

The principles of celestial mechanics extend beyond planets. Moons orbit planets, subject to the planet's gravity. Binary stars, two stars orbiting each other, are a testament to gravity's universal reach. Even galaxies, consisting of billions of stars, are held together by the collective gravitational attraction of their components. The dynamics within galaxies are incredibly complex, involving gravitational interactions between stars, gas clouds, and dark matter, a mysterious substance whose gravitational effects are observed but whose nature remains unknown.

Understanding orbital mechanics is crucial for various space exploration endeavors. Precise calculations of orbital trajectories are vital for launching satellites, planning interplanetary missions, and navigating spacecraft through the solar system. Careful consideration of gravitational forces is crucial to successfully maneuvering spacecraft around planets, moons, or other celestial bodies using gravitational assists or slingshots, techniques that exploit the gravitational pull of these bodies to accelerate or alter the spacecraft's trajectory. These techniques are often employed to reduce fuel consumption and extend the reach of missions to distant planets.

The concept of escape velocity is another key element in orbital mechanics. This is the minimum speed an object needs to escape the gravitational pull of a celestial body. If an object's speed exceeds its escape velocity, it will continue moving away from the body indefinitely; otherwise, it will eventually fall back under the influence of gravity. The escape velocity depends on the mass and radius of the celestial body; the more massive and compact the body, the higher the escape velocity.

The study of celestial mechanics is not solely concerned with the predictable movements of celestial bodies. It also incorporates the concept of perturbations, small disturbances in an object's orbit caused by gravitational influences from other celestial bodies. For example, the gravitational pull of Jupiter can slightly alter the orbits of asteroids in the asteroid belt. These subtle perturbations are often accounted for through complex mathematical models to accurately predict the future positions of celestial bodies. The study of these perturbations is especially important for long-term predictions of spacecraft trajectories and for understanding the stability of planetary systems over time.

The advances in observational astronomy and computational power have significantly expanded our ability to model and predict the movement of celestial bodies with unprecedented accuracy. Modern celestial mechanics relies heavily on sophisticated numerical simulations and advanced algorithms to model the complex gravitational interactions within stellar systems, galaxies, and even the entire universe. These simulations allow scientists to test different theories of gravity and explore various scenarios for the formation and evolution of celestial structures.

In conclusion, celestial mechanics is a cornerstone of our understanding of the universe. From the simple elegance of

Newton's Law of Universal Gravitation to the complex simulations of modern astrophysics, the principles of gravity and orbital mechanics provide a framework for interpreting the dynamic movements of celestial bodies, ranging from the planets in our solar system to the distant galaxies observed across the vast expanse of the cosmos. The continuing exploration and refinement of these principles will undoubtedly continue to enhance our understanding of the universe's evolution and our place within it.

Tools of the Trade Telescopes and Observatories

Our journey into the cosmos wouldn't be possible without the ingenious tools that allow us to peer into the vast expanse of space. These instruments, primarily telescopes and the observatories that house them, are the eyes and ears of astronomy, transforming faint glimmers of light and subtle radio waves into detailed images and invaluable data that reveal the secrets of the universe. Let's explore the fascinating world of these tools, examining their diverse types and capabilities.

The most familiar type of telescope is the optical telescope, designed to detect visible light, the same light our eyes perceive. These telescopes come in two primary designs: refracting and reflecting. Refracting telescopes, employing lenses to bend and focus light, were the earliest form of optical telescopes. Galileo's groundbreaking observations were made using a refracting telescope, showcasing its historical significance. However, refracting telescopes suffer from chromatic aberration, a color distortion caused by the different wavelengths of light refracting at slightly different angles. This limitation restricts their ability to achieve high resolution, especially for larger telescopes.

Reflecting telescopes, on the other hand, utilize mirrors to gather and focus light. This design overcomes the chromatic aberration issue of refracting telescopes and allows for the creation of much larger instruments, leading to significantly improved light-gathering power. The larger the mirror, the more light the telescope collects, enhancing its ability to detect fainter and more distant objects. Reflecting telescopes have become the dominant type used in modern astronomy, from ground-based observatories to space-based telescopes like the Hubble.

The construction of large reflecting telescopes presents significant engineering challenges. The mirrors need to be extremely precise, often requiring complex polishing techniques to achieve the necessary accuracy. Furthermore, the size and weight of the mirrors demand robust support structures to maintain their shape and prevent distortions caused by gravity. Modern reflecting telescopes frequently employ segmented mirrors, comprising numerous smaller mirror segments that work together to form a single large, reflective surface. This segmented design offers significant advantages in terms of cost, manufacturability, and transportability, particularly for extremely large telescopes.

Ground-based optical telescopes, while powerful, face limitations imposed by Earth's atmosphere. Atmospheric turbulence, caused by variations in air density and temperature, can distort the incoming light, blurring the images and reducing the resolution of observations. This atmospheric effect, known as "seeing," imposes a significant constraint on the quality of ground-based observations, particularly for high-resolution imaging. To mitigate these atmospheric effects, adaptive optics systems have been developed. These systems use deformable mirrors that constantly adjust their shape to compensate for the distortions caused by atmospheric turbulence, significantly improving the image quality.

To circumvent the limitations imposed by Earth's atmosphere, space telescopes were conceived and launched. Perhaps the most famous of these is the Hubble Space Telescope (HST), orbiting Earth high above the atmosphere. Free from atmospheric interference, HST has provided breathtakingly sharp images and revolutionized our understanding of the universe, allowing observation of objects previously obscured or too faint to be detected from Earth. However, even space telescopes face limitations.

Their size and complexity pose challenges in terms of launch, maintenance, and cost. The repairs and upgrades HST has undergone over its lifetime underscore this reality. Future space telescopes, like the James Webb Space Telescope (JWST), aim to overcome some of these limitations with advanced technologies and different observing wavelengths.

Beyond optical telescopes, other types of telescopes are used to explore the universe across a wider spectrum of electromagnetic radiation. Radio telescopes, for instance, detect radio waves emitted by celestial objects. Radio waves have much longer wavelengths than visible light, requiring large dish antennas to effectively collect them. The large collecting area of these antennas compensates for the lower energy of radio waves, making them particularly sensitive to radio emissions from distant galaxies, quasars, and pulsars.

Often, arrays of radio telescopes are used in conjunction, combining their signals to enhance the resolution through a technique known as interferometry. This allows radio astronomers to obtain images with remarkable detail and angular resolution, often surpassing what can be achieved with optical telescopes.

The Very Large Array (VLA) in New Mexico is a prime example of a radio telescope array. Its 27 antennas spread across a vast area work together to create an exceptionally powerful and versatile radio astronomy observatory. This array has been instrumental in various discoveries, ranging from the mapping of distant galaxies to the detection of molecules in interstellar space. The Event Horizon Telescope (EHT), a global network of radio telescopes, achieved the remarkable feat of imaging the black hole at the center of the galaxy M87, a feat thought impossible just a few decades ago.

X-ray and gamma-ray telescopes are used to observe the highest-energy forms of electromagnetic radiation. X-rays and gamma rays are highly penetrating, requiring specialized detectors to capture them. These telescopes often employ sophisticated techniques to focus and detect these high- energy photons, providing information about the most energetic phenomena in the universe, such as supernovae, active galactic nuclei, and neutron star collisions. These

high-energy observations reveal aspects of the universe that are invisible to optical and radio telescopes.

Observatories play a crucial role in the functioning of these telescopes. These facilities provide the infrastructure needed to house, operate, and maintain the telescopes, as well as offering the necessary support systems for astronomers to carry out their research. Many observatories are located in remote locations with exceptionally dark skies, minimizing light pollution and maximizing observing conditions. The choice of location is paramount, considering factors like altitude (reducing atmospheric effects), atmospheric stability, and remoteness from urban light sources. Modern observatories are equipped with sophisticated computer systems that control the telescopes, acquire data, and process images.

Data analysis forms the crucial final step in astronomical research. The massive amounts of data collected by telescopes and observatories require sophisticated computational techniques and algorithms for processing, analysis, and interpretation. Astronomers utilize advanced software and powerful computing resources to sift through the data, extract meaningful information, and construct models to understand the universe. This process involves techniques such as image processing, spectral analysis, and statistical modeling, often using machine learning algorithms to aid in pattern recognition and data interpretation.

The tools of space science, from optical telescopes to radio and X-ray observatories, are continually evolving through technological advancements. Improvements in mirror technology, detector sensitivity, and data analysis techniques are pushing the boundaries of our observational capabilities. The development of larger telescopes, more sensitive detectors, and advanced data analysis methods continuously enhances our ability to explore the universe in greater detail and precision. The discoveries we have made, and those yet to come, are testament to the power and ingenuity of these tools. As technology progresses, the secrets of the universe will further unfold, providing an ever-deeper understanding of our place in the cosmos.

The History of Space Exploration

Our understanding of the universe, as revealed by the powerful tools of modern astronomy, rests on a foundation built over millennia of observation and exploration. Long before the invention of the telescope, humans looked to the heavens, charting the movements of celestial bodies and weaving intricate myths to explain their perceived patterns. Ancient civilizations, from the Babylonians to the Egyptians, the Greeks to the Mayans, meticulously tracked the positions of stars and planets, developing sophisticated calendars and astronomical systems that served both practical and ritualistic purposes. These early observations, though limited by the naked eye, laid the groundwork for future scientific advancements.

The invention of the telescope in the early 17th century marked a pivotal moment in the history of astronomy. While the precise attribution of its invention remains debated, Galileo Galilei's pioneering use of a telescope to observe the celestial realm revolutionized our understanding of the cosmos. His observations of the Moon's surface, revealing its craters and mountains, challenged the prevailing geocentric model of the universe. His discoveries of Jupiter's moons and the phases of Venus provided compelling evidence supporting the heliocentric model proposed by Copernicus, placing the Sun, not the Earth, at the center of our solar system. This shift in perspective fundamentally altered our place in the universe.

The subsequent centuries witnessed a steady progression in telescope technology, leading to the development of larger and more powerful instruments. Improvements in lens grinding and mirror polishing techniques allowed astronomers to observe fainter and more distant objects. The construction of observatories in strategic locations, often atop mountains to minimize atmospheric interference, further enhanced observation capabilities. The use of photography in astronomy, beginning in the mid-19th century, revolutionized data acquisition, enabling astronomers to record and analyze celestial events with unprecedented detail and precision. This led to significant discoveries, including the identification of new celestial bodies and the mapping of nebulae and galaxies.

The 20th century ushered in the Space Age, a period of unprecedented exploration and discovery beyond Earth's atmosphere. The launch of Sputnik 1 by the Soviet Union in 1957 marked the beginning of the space race, a geopolitical competition between the United States and the Soviet Union that spurred rapid advancements in rocket technology and space exploration. This competition fostered remarkable progress in our understanding of space, pushing technological boundaries and inspiring generations of scientists and engineers.

The early space missions focused primarily on Earth orbit and the collection of data about our planet and its environment. However, the ambition of reaching the Moon quickly emerged as a central goal of the space race. The United States' Apollo program, culminating in the Apollo 11 mission in 1969, marked a pivotal moment in human history

—the first time human beings set foot on another celestial body. The Apollo missions not only fulfilled a national ambition but also generated a wealth of scientific data about the Moon's geology, composition, and history. The astronauts brought back lunar samples, which continue to be studied today, providing invaluable insights into the early solar system.

Beyond the human exploration of the Moon, the latter half of the 20th century and the beginning of the 21st saw an expansion of robotic exploration throughout our solar system. Space probes were launched to explore the planets, moons, asteroids, and comets, transmitting back stunning images and data that significantly broadened our understanding of these celestial objects. Missions such as the Voyager program, which sent probes to explore the outer planets, revealed the diversity and complexity of our solar system. Similarly, missions to Mars, such as the Mars Pathfinder and Curiosity rovers, provided close-up views of the Martian surface, analyzing its composition and searching for evidence of past or present life. These robotic missions have become increasingly sophisticated, incorporating advanced technologies and instruments to expand our understanding of the universe.

The development of space telescopes marked another watershed moment in space exploration. Unlike ground- based telescopes, space telescopes operate above Earth's atmosphere, eliminating the distortion caused by atmospheric turbulence. The Hubble Space Telescope, launched in 1990, revolutionized astronomy with its breathtakingly clear images of distant galaxies, nebulae, and planets. Its observations have provided invaluable data, leading to significant advancements in our understanding of the universe's expansion, the formation of galaxies, and the life cycles of stars. The Hubble's success paved the way for more advanced space telescopes, such as the James Webb Space Telescope (JWST), which is equipped with even more powerful instruments capable of observing further into the universe's past.

The history of space exploration is not only a story of technological innovation but also a narrative of human ambition, perseverance, and international collaboration. The space race, though initially driven by geopolitical competition, ultimately spurred immense progress in science and technology. The subsequent decades have witnessed a shift towards more international cooperation in space exploration, with numerous joint missions involving scientists and engineers from various countries. The International Space Station (ISS), a collaborative project involving several nations, serves as a testament to this international collaboration, providing a platform for scientific research and technological development in space.

Looking ahead, the future of space exploration promises even greater discoveries. Plans for future missions to Mars, including the possibility of sending humans to the red planet, represent ambitious goals that will require further advancements in technology and international cooperation.

The search for extraterrestrial life, a long-standing quest, is also gaining momentum, with new missions and instruments designed to detect biosignatures on other planets or moons. Furthermore, the development of new telescope technologies and observational techniques continues to push the boundaries of our understanding of the universe, enabling us to probe deeper into its mysteries. The ongoing exploration of space continues to capture the imagination of humanity, driving our quest to unravel the universe's secrets. From ancient stargazers to modern-day astronauts and scientists, our journey into the cosmos reflects our innate curiosity and our persistent striving to understand our place within this vast and wondrous universe. The remarkable achievements of the past inspire us to continue exploring, discovering, and pushing the boundaries of human knowledge, ensuring that our journey into space remains a testament to human ingenuity and our endless fascination with the cosmos. The relentless pursuit of knowledge about the universe, a pursuit driven by curiosity and the pursuit of understanding, has been fueled by technological advancements, international collaborations, and the unwavering dedication of countless scientists, engineers, and astronauts. This ongoing exploration promises further breakthroughs and an ever- deepening understanding of our place in the universe. The legacy of past explorations inspires us to venture further, pushing the boundaries of human knowledge, technological innovation, and our capacity for awe and wonder.

Earths Unique Characteristics and Habitability

Our journey through the cosmos has brought us to a profound understanding of the universe's vastness and the remarkable diversity of celestial bodies within it. Yet, amidst this grand tapestry of stars, galaxies, and nebulae, one planet stands out as uniquely special: Earth. Having explored the history of our astronomical understanding and the technological leaps that propelled us into the space age, we now turn our focus inward, to the intricate details of our own home planet and the remarkable confluence of factors that make it capable of supporting life as we know it.

The Earth's habitability is not merely a matter of chance; it is a result of a delicate balance of factors operating over billions of years. Firstly, its position within the solar system is paramount. Situated within the "Goldilocks zone," or circumstellar habitable zone, Earth orbits the Sun at a distance that allows for the existence of liquid water on its surface. If Earth were significantly closer to the Sun, water would exist only as vapor, creating a runaway greenhouse effect similar to what we observe on Venus. Conversely, if it were farther away, all water would be frozen, rendering the planet uninhabitable. This precise orbital distance, a consequence of the Sun's mass and the initial conditions of the solar system's formation, provides the fundamental precondition for life.

Beyond its advantageous orbital position, Earth's atmosphere plays a crucial role in maintaining a habitable environment. Composed primarily of nitrogen and oxygen, the atmosphere acts as a protective shield, absorbing harmful ultraviolet radiation from the Sun and regulating the planet's temperature. The greenhouse effect, often portrayed as a solely negative consequence of human activity, is in fact essential for maintaining Earth's average temperature at a level conducive to liquid water. While the increase in greenhouse gases due to human activities poses a serious threat, the natural greenhouse effect is crucial for life. The atmospheric composition has evolved dramatically over billions of years, initially being primarily composed of volcanic gases. The slow but dramatic transition to an oxygen-rich atmosphere was a pivotal moment in Earth's history, paving the way for the evolution of complex life forms. The delicate balance of gases in Earth's atmosphere is maintained by a complex interplay of geological and biological processes, highlighting the intricate interconnectedness of Earth's systems.

The presence of liquid water on Earth's surface is another critical factor supporting life. Water acts as a universal solvent, facilitating numerous biochemical reactions essential for life. It is crucial for transporting nutrients within organisms, regulating temperature, and providing a medium for the transport of materials. The vast oceans covering approximately 71% of Earth's surface serve as a massive heat reservoir, moderating temperature fluctuations and influencing weather patterns. The hydrological cycle, driven by solar energy, ensures the continuous circulation of water between the oceans, atmosphere, and land, maintaining a dynamic equilibrium that is vital for the Earth's climate system. The availability of liquid water, both on the surface and within the subsurface, has shaped the course of evolution, determining the distribution and diversity of life on Earth.

Geological processes have also played a significant role in shaping Earth's habitable environment. Plate tectonics, a unique feature of our planet, drives the recycling of Earth's crustal material, creating a dynamic landscape that continuously shapes the environment. This process is fundamental for regulating the concentration of carbon dioxide in the atmosphere. Volcanic activity, driven by plate tectonics, releases greenhouse gases into the atmosphere, influencing the climate. Simultaneously, weathering and erosion, processes that break down rocks and transport them to the oceans, remove carbon dioxide from the atmosphere, acting as a natural thermostat. This constant interplay between volcanism and weathering is a crucial component in regulating Earth's long-term climate stability, preventing extreme temperature variations that would threaten life.

The unique geological history of Earth also shaped the availability of essential elements for life. The formation of continents and oceans, driven by plate tectonics, provided diverse habitats for life to evolve. The concentration of minerals within the crust and oceans has influenced the development of biological processes. The formation of sedimentary rocks, rich in organic matter, has served as a repository for past life forms, providing invaluable insights into the history of life on Earth. The interplay of geological processes, and the resulting diverse geological formations, is fundamental to the planet's ability to sustain life.

Beyond its physical characteristics, Earth's biosphere, the zone of life that encompasses all living organisms, plays a crucial role in maintaining habitability. The biosphere is not simply a passive recipient of Earth's physical environment; it actively shapes it. Photosynthesis, the process by which plants and other organisms convert solar energy into chemical energy, has profoundly influenced Earth's atmosphere, increasing the concentration of oxygen and reducing the concentration of carbon dioxide. Biological processes involved in weathering and erosion further regulate atmospheric composition and climate. The complex interactions within the biosphere, the interplay between different species, and their relationship with the physical environment, have contributed to the resilience and stability of Earth's life-support systems.

Furthermore, Earth's magnetic field acts as a crucial shield, deflecting charged particles from the Sun (solar wind) and cosmic rays. Without this magnetic field, our atmosphere would be gradually eroded by the solar wind, leading to a loss of water and a dramatic shift in the environment. The magnetic field is generated by the planet's liquid iron core, a process known as dynamo effect, driven by convection currents within the core. This inherent process provides a fundamental form of protection which is crucial for the continuation of life.

The exceptional habitability of Earth is not simply a product of a single factor, but rather a delicate and complex interplay of several interacting elements. Its position within the solar system, atmospheric composition, presence of liquid water, geological processes, and the dynamic biosphere work together in a remarkable symphony of environmental factors, creating a unique environment capable of sustaining an incredibly diverse range of life. Understanding this intricate interplay is paramount, not only for appreciating the wonder of our planet but also for addressing the current environmental challenges we face and ensuring the continued habitability of Earth for future generations. Our planet's unique characteristics, painstakingly developed over billions of years, highlight the preciousness of this life-sustaining oasis in the vast expanse of the cosmos. As we explore the universe in search of other habitable worlds, we should continually reflect upon the remarkable conditions that have allowed life to flourish here on Earth and strive to understand, appreciate and preserve this fragile balance. The future of life on Earth depends on our ability to comprehend and safeguard the intricate network of environmental interactions that have made our planet the vibrant, diverse, and life-filled world it is today.

Earths Atmosphere and Climate

Earth's atmosphere is a dynamic and complex system, a crucial component in the planet's habitability. It's not just a thin layer of air; it's a multi-layered structure, each layer playing a distinct role in shaping our environment. The lowest layer, the troposphere, extends from the Earth's surface to an altitude of roughly 7 to 10 kilometers, varying with latitude and season. This is where most of our weather occurs, where clouds form, and where we experience the daily fluctuations in temperature and pressure. The troposphere contains approximately 80% of the atmosphere's mass and is where the majority of atmospheric gases reside – primarily nitrogen (78%), oxygen (21%), and trace amounts of argon, carbon dioxide, and other gases. The proportion of these gases is critical, as each plays a specific role in the Earth's climate system. The relative abundance of oxygen, a product of billions of years of photosynthetic activity, supports the complex life forms that populate our planet. The concentration of carbon dioxide, while relatively small, plays a disproportionately large role in regulating global temperatures through the greenhouse effect.

Above the troposphere lies the stratosphere, extending from roughly 10 to 50 kilometers. This layer is characterized by a temperature inversion, meaning the temperature increases with altitude. This is largely due to the absorption of ultraviolet (UV) radiation from the Sun by the ozone layer, a region within the stratosphere containing a higher concentration of ozone (O_3) molecules. This ozone layer acts as a vital shield, protecting life on Earth from harmful UV radiation, which can cause damage to DNA and other biological molecules. The depletion of the ozone layer due to human-made chemicals like chlorofluorocarbons (CFCs) highlighted the fragility of this protective shield and prompted international efforts to mitigate further damage through agreements like the Montreal Protocol.

Beyond the stratosphere is the mesosphere, extending to approximately 85 kilometers. In this layer, the temperature decreases with increasing altitude, reaching the coldest temperatures in the Earth's atmosphere. Meteors burn up in this layer, creating the familiar "shooting star" phenomenon. Above the mesosphere lies the thermosphere, extending to several hundred kilometers. In the thermosphere, the temperature increases with altitude due to the absorption of high-energy solar radiation. The International Space Station orbits in this layer, as does the majority of the satellites that enable our modern communication systems and Earth observation technologies. The ionosphere, a region of the upper atmosphere encompassing parts of the thermosphere and mesosphere, is characterized by the ionization of gases due to solar radiation. This layer plays a critical role in radio wave propagation, reflecting radio waves back to Earth, enabling long-distance communication.

Finally, the exosphere represents the outermost layer of the atmosphere, gradually transitioning into the vacuum of space. The boundary between the exosphere and space is not clearly defined, but it's generally considered to start at an altitude of around 500 to 1000 kilometers. The exosphere is extremely tenuous, with the atmospheric gases becoming increasingly sparse. This layer is sparsely populated with extremely light gas particles, and they may escape from the Earth's gravitational pull, adding complexity to the dynamics of the atmosphere.

The composition of the Earth's atmosphere, and its layered structure, is fundamental to regulating the planet's climate. The greenhouse effect, often viewed with apprehension due to its connection to climate change, is a naturally occurring process that plays a critical role in maintaining Earth's temperature within a habitable range. Certain atmospheric gases, known as greenhouse gases, trap heat radiated by the Earth's surface, preventing it from escaping into space. This trapping of heat is essential for maintaining a global average temperature that allows for the presence of liquid water.

Water vapor (H_2O) is the most potent greenhouse gas, but its concentration is largely determined by the temperature itself. Carbon dioxide (CO_2), methane (CH_4), nitrous oxide (N_2O), and ozone (O_3) are other significant greenhouse gases.

While the natural greenhouse effect is essential for life, human activities have significantly increased the concentrations of greenhouse gases in the atmosphere, primarily through the burning of fossil fuels, deforestation, and agricultural practices. This increased concentration leads to an enhanced greenhouse effect, causing a gradual increase in global temperatures. This phenomenon is widely recognized as climate change and is manifesting itself in various ways, including rising sea levels, more frequent and intense heatwaves, changes in precipitation patterns, and the increased frequency and intensity of extreme weather events. The consequences of climate change are far-reaching, affecting ecosystems, human societies, and the global economy.

Understanding Earth's atmospheric science is crucial to addressing the challenges posed by climate change. The monitoring of atmospheric composition, the study of climate models, and the development of mitigation and adaptation strategies are vital in safeguarding the planet's habitability.

Advanced technologies, including satellites, weather stations, and sophisticated climate models, provide invaluable data for monitoring atmospheric changes and making predictions about future climate scenarios. International collaboration is critical in coordinating research, sharing data, and implementing global policies aimed at mitigating climate change and its impacts. The transition towards renewable energy sources, the development of carbon capture technologies, and the adoption of sustainable agricultural practices are crucial steps in reducing greenhouse gas emissions and mitigating the effects of climate change.

The impact of climate change is already being felt worldwide, and its long-term effects could have catastrophic consequences. Understanding the intricate workings of our atmosphere, from the protective ozone layer to the complex interactions among greenhouse gases, is essential to develop effective strategies to curb climate change. This includes not just reducing emissions but also adapting to the changes that are already underway. Investing in infrastructure that can withstand extreme weather events, developing drought- resistant crops, and improving coastal defenses are crucial adaptations that can help communities cope with the impacts of climate change. The challenge of climate change requires a multi-pronged approach involving scientific research, technological innovation, policy changes, and individual actions. Only through collective global efforts can we strive towards a future where the Earth's atmosphere remains a stable and life-sustaining environment for generations to come. The study of Earth's atmosphere isn't merely an academic pursuit; it's an essential part of our efforts to ensure the future of our planet.

Earths Oceans and Their Mysteries

Our understanding of Earth's systems wouldn't be complete without a deep dive into its magnificent oceans. Covering over 70% of our planet's surface, these vast bodies of water are far more than just picturesque landscapes; they are integral to the Earth's climate regulation, the cradle of life, and a powerful force shaping our weather patterns. The oceans, a continuous, interconnected global system, influence everything from the air we breathe to the food we eat. Their sheer scale is breathtaking; imagine a volume of water so immense that it holds approximately 97% of all the planet's water. This massive reservoir plays a critical role in moderating global temperatures, absorbing vast quantities of solar radiation and distributing heat around the globe through ocean currents. These currents, driven by temperature differences, salinity variations, and wind patterns, act as a massive planetary conveyor belt, transporting warm water from the tropics towards the poles and cooler water back towards the equator, influencing climate zones across the planet. The Gulf Stream, for instance, is a prime example of this, bringing relatively warm water to the North Atlantic, significantly moderating the climate of Western Europe. Without this ocean current regulation, the climate across the globe would be significantly different and harsher.

The oceans are not static; they are dynamic systems, perpetually in motion. Waves, driven by wind, are a constant feature of the ocean surface, constantly exchanging energy between the atmosphere and the ocean. Tides, the rhythmic rise and fall of sea levels, are influenced by the gravitational pull of the moon and the sun, and their patterns are complex, varying across the globe depending on coastal geography and celestial mechanics. These tidal forces play a crucial role in shaping coastal ecosystems and influencing the distribution of marine life. Ocean currents, waves, and tides combine to create a complex and ever-changing ocean environment, constantly shaping and reshaping coastlines and contributing to the erosion and deposition of sediments.

Beyond the surface, the oceans conceal a world of mystery and wonder. The deep ocean, extending to the crushing pressures of the hadal zone, remains largely unexplored.

Technological advancements in submersible vehicles and remotely operated vehicles (ROVs) are slowly unveiling the secrets of these extreme environments. Imagine the pressure; at the deepest point in the ocean, the Mariana Trench, the pressure is more than 1,000 times greater than at sea level – an immense force that necessitates specially designed equipment to explore. This pressure has led to the evolution of unique and remarkable adaptations in the creatures inhabiting these depths. Bioluminescence, the production and emission of light by living organisms, is a common phenomenon in the deep ocean, enabling communication, hunting, and defense in the near-total darkness. The pressure also affects the physical properties of water itself, altering the density and behavior of aquatic life forms in profound ways.

The deep ocean is home to a rich diversity of life, often adapted to these extreme conditions in surprising ways. Hydrothermal vents, fissures in the ocean floor releasing superheated water rich in minerals, support thriving ecosystems even in the absence of sunlight. These vents sustain chemosynthetic bacteria, which form the base of the food chain, supporting entire communities of organisms that have evolved to withstand extreme temperatures and pressure. Giant tube worms, blind shrimp, and other unusual creatures populate these unique habitats, offering profound insights into the resilience and adaptability of life. Exploring these deep-sea ecosystems provides valuable data for understanding the origins of life and the potential for life beyond Earth. There's ongoing research on extremophiles – organisms that thrive in extreme environments such as these hydrothermal vents – that could hold the key to understanding life's possibilities in other parts of our solar system or beyond.

The ocean floor itself is a complex and dynamic landscape, with vast mountain ranges, deep trenches, and volcanic activity shaping its topography. The mid-ocean ridges, underwater mountain ranges formed by volcanic activity, represent some of the Earth's most geologically active regions. These ridges, extending for thousands of kilometers across the ocean floor, are sites where new oceanic crust is created through the process of seafloor spreading, a fundamental process in plate tectonics. The study of these geological formations provides vital clues to understanding the Earth's geological history, and the processes that have shaped our planet over millions of years. Subduction zones, where one tectonic plate slides beneath another, also contribute to creating dramatic changes in the seabed topography, causing earthquakes and tsunamis with far- reaching consequences. The study of these deep ocean geological processes helps us better understand and prepare for the powerful forces acting beneath our feet.

The oceans' influence extends far beyond their physical boundaries. They play a crucial role in regulating the Earth's climate, absorbing carbon dioxide from the atmosphere and influencing global weather patterns. The oceans act as a massive carbon sink, absorbing a significant portion of the excess carbon dioxide produced by human activities. This absorption helps to mitigate the effects of climate change, but it also comes at a cost. The increasing absorption of carbon dioxide leads to ocean acidification, altering the chemistry of the oceans and negatively affecting marine life, particularly those with calcium carbonate shells or skeletons. Coral reefs, for example, are highly vulnerable to ocean acidification, as the acidification makes it difficult for corals to build and maintain their skeletons.

The oceans are also a significant source of oxygen, with phytoplankton, microscopic marine organisms, producing a significant portion of the oxygen we breathe. These single- celled organisms conduct photosynthesis, harnessing the energy of the sun to convert carbon dioxide and water into energy and oxygen. Their contribution to our atmosphere is a critical reminder of the interconnectedness of Earth's systems and the oceans' vital role in supporting life on our planet.

Disruptions to ocean ecosystems, whether through pollution, overfishing, or climate change, can have far-reaching consequences on this oxygen production and its effect on the global environment.

Beyond their ecological significance, the oceans have profoundly impacted human history and culture. Throughout history, oceans have served as highways for exploration, trade, and migration, connecting distant cultures and civilizations. Oceans have been a source of sustenance, providing food and resources for coastal communities for millennia. Coastal communities have developed unique cultural traditions tied to the rhythms of the tides, the cycles of the seasons, and the abundance of marine life. Yet, the very same oceans that have sustained us for so long are now threatened by human activities. Pollution, overfishing, and climate change pose significant threats to marine ecosystems, jeopardizing the health of the oceans and the well-being of human populations that depend on them.

The mysteries of the deep ocean continue to challenge and inspire scientists, pushing the boundaries of exploration and technological innovation. The development of advanced submersibles, ROVs, and autonomous underwater vehicles (AUVs) is allowing scientists to explore previously inaccessible regions of the ocean, revealing new species, geological formations, and ecological interactions. The study of marine microorganisms, many of which still remain unidentified, is revealing new insights into the biodiversity and ecological functions of the oceans. And through the use of advanced genetic sequencing, scientists are beginning to unlock the secrets of the evolution of marine life and their adaptations to the extreme pressures and temperatures of the deep sea.

The oceans' health is inextricably linked to the health of our planet. Protecting and preserving these vast and vital ecosystems is not just an environmental imperative; it is essential for the future of humanity. The continued exploration and study of Earth's oceans are critical to developing effective strategies for conservation, sustainable resource management, and mitigating the impacts of climate change. It is a crucial aspect of our broader effort to ensure the well-being of our planet and its inhabitants. Our understanding of these immense and dynamic bodies of water is constantly evolving, and each new discovery underscores the importance of continued research, technological innovation, and global cooperation in safeguarding our planet's oceans for generations to come.

The journey into the depths of the ocean is a journey into the very heart of our planet, a world teeming with life, mystery, and immense potential.

Earths Interior Structure and Geological Processes

Having explored the vast and dynamic oceans that cover much of our planet's surface, we now delve beneath the waves, into the very heart of Earth itself. Our home planet is not a monolithic sphere; it's a complex, layered system, a dynamic engine of geological activity that has shaped the surface we inhabit and continues to do so today.

Understanding Earth's internal structure and the geological processes that govern it is crucial to comprehending our planet's history, predicting future events like earthquakes and volcanic eruptions, and appreciating the intricate interconnectedness of Earth's various systems.

The Earth's interior is far from uniform. Instead, it's structured in a series of concentric layers, each with distinct physical properties and chemical compositions. The deepest layer is the core, a region of immense pressure and temperature. This core is further divided into two parts: a solid inner core, primarily composed of iron and nickel, and a liquid outer core, also largely iron and nickel, but in a molten state. The movement of this liquid outer core, driven by Earth's rotation and convection currents, generates our planet's magnetic field, a protective shield that deflects harmful solar radiation and charged particles from the sun. This magnetic field is crucial for life on Earth, as it prevents the stripping away of our atmosphere by the solar wind, a constant stream of charged particles emanating from the sun. The magnetic field's strength and its configuration are not constant, constantly fluctuating and shifting, a phenomenon studied intensely by geophysicists.

Surrounding the core is the mantle, a much thicker layer primarily composed of silicate rocks. Unlike the core, the mantle is not completely molten; instead, it behaves like a highly viscous fluid, capable of slow, plastic deformation over geological timescales. This is a key aspect of the theory of plate tectonics, which we will explore in detail later. The mantle is also responsible for the transfer of heat from the Earth's core to the surface, driving convection currents that power many geological processes. These convection currents are like a vast, slow-moving river of molten rock within the Earth, constantly pushing and pulling the tectonic plates above them. The immense pressure and temperature gradients within the mantle lead to the development of complex convection patterns that are not fully understood and remain an active area of research. Some of the most insightful observations come from monitoring seismic waves which reflect and refract as they pass through different layers, providing valuable data on the mantle's composition and structure. The exact nature of convection currents and their variability within the mantle remains a subject of ongoing scientific investigation, using sophisticated computer models combined with seismological data to reconstruct the dynamics of the Earth's interior.

The outermost layer is the crust, the relatively thin and brittle shell on which we live. This layer is significantly less dense than the mantle and the core. The crust is divided into two types: oceanic crust, which forms the ocean floor and is primarily composed of basalt, a dark-colored volcanic rock; and continental crust, which forms the continents and is primarily composed of granite, a lighter-colored igneous rock. The oceanic crust is much thinner than the continental crust, typically around 5-10 kilometers thick, whereas the continental crust can reach thicknesses of up to 70 kilometers in some mountainous regions. The contrast in thickness and composition between these two types of crust plays a significant role in plate tectonics and the formation of mountain ranges and ocean basins. The study of the chemical composition of rocks from both oceanic and continental crust is crucial for understanding the formation and evolution of these distinct parts of the Earth's surface. In recent years, advancements in isotope geochemistry have provided significant insights into the age and origin of these rocks, further illuminating the long and complex geological history of our planet.

The theory of plate tectonics revolutionized our understanding of Earth's geological processes. This theory proposes that the Earth's lithosphere, the rigid outermost shell comprising the crust and the uppermost part of the mantle, is broken into a series of large and small plates that are constantly moving, albeit very slowly, relative to each other. These plates float on the semi-molten asthenosphere, a region within the upper mantle that behaves in a more ductile manner. The movement of these plates is driven by the heat emanating from the Earth's core, creating convection currents in the mantle. This constant movement of plates is responsible for many of Earth's most dramatic geological features.

The interaction between these plates results in three main types of plate boundaries: divergent boundaries, convergent boundaries, and transform boundaries. At divergent boundaries, two plates move apart, creating new oceanic crust through a process called seafloor spreading. This process occurs primarily at mid-ocean ridges, underwater mountain ranges that extend for thousands of kilometers across the ocean floor. As the plates separate, magma from the mantle rises to fill the gap, cooling and solidifying to form new oceanic crust. This continuous creation of new oceanic crust helps to explain the age distribution of the oceanic crust, with younger crust found near mid-ocean ridges and older crust found farther away. The study of these mid-ocean ridges provides crucial evidence for the theory of plate tectonics. Precise measurements of the age of the seafloor, obtained from paleomagnetic studies and radiometric dating of rock samples, strongly corroborate the predictions of the theory.

At convergent boundaries, two plates collide. The outcome of this collision depends on the type of plates involved. If one plate is oceanic and the other is continental, the denser oceanic plate subducts, or slides beneath, the continental plate. This process creates deep ocean trenches, volcanic mountain ranges, and powerful earthquakes. The subduction zone, where the oceanic plate descends into the mantle, is a site of intense geological activity. The frictional forces generated during subduction can lead to the melting of the subducting plate and the surrounding mantle material. This molten material then rises to the surface, forming volcanic arcs, chains of volcanoes parallel to the subduction zone.

The Andes Mountains in South America are a prime example of a volcanic arc formed at a convergent plate boundary. The same process is at work, though on a smaller scale, in volcanic island arcs such as the Japanese archipelago.

If both colliding plates are oceanic, the denser plate will subduct beneath the other, forming volcanic island arcs. If both plates are continental, neither plate subducts easily due to their comparable densities, resulting in the collision of tectonic plates and the formation of large mountain ranges such as the Himalayas. The immense forces involved in such collisions cause widespread deformation of the crust, including folding, faulting, and uplift. The collision between the Indian and Eurasian plates is a prime example of continental-continental convergence, leading to the formation of the Himalayas and the Tibetan Plateau, the highest mountain range and highest plateau on Earth. The ongoing collision continues to uplift these landforms, generating strong earthquakes in the region.

At transform boundaries, two plates slide past each other horizontally. These boundaries are often characterized by frequent earthquakes, as the plates get locked and then suddenly slip, releasing enormous amounts of energy. The San Andreas Fault in California is a well-known example of a transform boundary. The movement along transform boundaries can cause significant disruption to the Earth's surface, resulting in offsetting of landforms and the creation of linear valleys.

The geological processes occurring at plate boundaries have profound effects on Earth's surface. Volcanoes, formed by the eruption of molten rock (magma) from the Earth's interior, are a dramatic manifestation of these processes.

Volcanic activity can release enormous amounts of gases and ash into the atmosphere, impacting the climate, while volcanic eruptions can cause devastating destruction.

Earthquakes, sudden releases of energy along faults, can trigger tsunamis, landslides, and widespread damage. The understanding of earthquake mechanisms, specifically the processes of stress accumulation, fault slip, and seismic wave propagation, is vital for improved seismic hazard assessment and mitigation strategies. Advancements in earthquake early warning systems provide crucial time to respond to impending earthquake activity, minimizing casualties.

The formation of mountains is another consequence of plate tectonics. Mountain ranges can arise from various tectonic processes, including the collision of continents, volcanic activity, and the uplift of the Earth's crust along fault lines. The interplay of tectonic forces, erosion, and other geological processes contributes to the formation and evolution of complex mountain systems.

In conclusion, Earth's internal structure and the geological processes that shape it are intricately connected. From the churning liquid outer core to the moving tectonic plates of the lithosphere, our planet is a dynamic system constantly evolving. Understanding this dynamic interplay is key to comprehending the processes that have shaped our planet over billions of years and to preparing for the geological events that will continue to shape our future. The ongoing study of Earth's interior, using techniques like seismology, geochemistry, and advanced computer modeling, continues to reveal new insights into the workings of our planet, advancing our capacity for prediction and mitigation of natural hazards. The investigation into the Earth's intricate system continues, promising ever-more detailed understanding of the processes that have shaped and continue to shape our remarkable home.

Life on Earth Evolution and Biodiversity

Having established the dynamic geological foundation of our planet, we now turn our attention to the breathtaking tapestry of life that has evolved upon it. Earth's remarkable history isn't just a story of shifting continents and erupting volcanoes; it's also a saga of life's tenacious struggle for survival, adaptation, and diversification. From the simplest single-celled organisms to the complex ecosystems teeming with biodiversity today, life has relentlessly shaped and been shaped by the planet's physical environment.

The story begins billions of years ago, in a vastly different world than the one we know. The early Earth was a hostile place, characterized by intense volcanic activity, a toxic atmosphere lacking free oxygen, and frequent bombardments from space. Yet, somehow, life emerged. The exact mechanisms remain a subject of ongoing scientific investigation, but prevailing hypotheses suggest that life originated in hydrothermal vents on the ocean floor or in shallow pools of water. These environments provided the necessary chemical ingredients and energy sources for the formation of the first self-replicating molecules, the precursors to life as we know it.

These initial life forms were simple, single-celled prokaryotes – organisms lacking a defined nucleus. They were extremophiles, thriving in extreme conditions that would be lethal to most life today. Over eons, these early prokaryotes evolved, diversifying into various forms and adapting to different environments. A pivotal moment in the history of life was the evolution of photosynthesis, the process by which organisms harness sunlight to convert carbon dioxide and water into energy. This innovation not only provided a new energy source for life but also had a profound impact on the planet's atmosphere. Photosynthetic organisms, primarily cyanobacteria, began to release vast quantities of oxygen into the atmosphere, gradually transforming it from a reducing environment to an oxidizing one. This "Great Oxidation Event" paved the way for the evolution of more complex forms of life, including those that could utilize oxygen for respiration, a much more efficient way of generating energy.

The rise of oxygen led to the Cambrian explosion, a period of rapid diversification of life that occurred roughly 540 million years ago. The fossil record from this era reveals an astonishing array of new body plans and forms, representing a dramatic increase in both the complexity and diversity of life. This explosion of life wasn't a sudden event; rather, it represents an acceleration in the rate of evolution driven by multiple factors, including the increased availability of oxygen, the evolution of new genetic mechanisms, and changes in the environment. Among the notable developments during the Cambrian explosion was the evolution of hard body parts such as shells and exoskeletons, which are more readily preserved in the fossil record, leading to a more complete picture of life during this period.

Following the Cambrian explosion, life continued to evolve and diversify, giving rise to an astonishing array of organisms. Plants colonized the land, followed by animals, adapting to a new and challenging environment. Over millions of years, life continuously shaped the Earth's environment and, in turn, was shaped by it. The evolution of land plants, for example, dramatically altered the landscape, leading to soil formation and increased erosion. The subsequent evolution of animals led to further environmental changes, like the creation of burrows and the transformation of forests.

The principles of natural selection, as articulated by Charles Darwin, are fundamental to our understanding of evolution. Natural selection is a process where organisms with traits better suited to their environment are more likely to survive and reproduce, passing on those advantageous traits to their offspring. This process, operating over vast spans of time, leads to the gradual adaptation of species to their surroundings. Numerous examples illustrate the power of natural selection, from the camouflage of insects to the streamlined bodies of aquatic animals. The evolution of antibiotic resistance in bacteria is a stark reminder of the ongoing interplay between life and its environment, highlighting the adaptive power of natural selection even in the face of human intervention.

The diversity of life on Earth is staggering. Ecologists categorize organisms into hierarchical systems, from species to ecosystems. A species is defined as a group of organisms that can interbreed and produce fertile offspring. Species are grouped into genera, families, orders, classes, phyla, kingdoms, and domains, reflecting their evolutionary relationships. The sheer number of species on Earth is estimated to be in the millions, with many still undiscovered. This biodiversity is not evenly distributed across the planet; rather, it varies considerably depending on factors like climate, geography, and the availability of resources.

Ecosystems are complex communities of interacting organisms and their physical environment. Each ecosystem has a unique structure and function, defined by the types of organisms that inhabit it and the relationships between them. Forests, grasslands, deserts, and oceans are all examples of distinct ecosystems, each supporting a wide array of species. The interactions within an ecosystem can be intricate, with intricate food webs linking producers, consumers, and decomposers. The delicate balance of these interactions is crucial for maintaining the stability and resilience of the ecosystem.

Human activities have had a profound and often detrimental impact on biodiversity. Habitat destruction, pollution, climate change, and overexploitation of resources are all significant drivers of species extinction and ecosystem degradation. The rate of species extinction is now estimated to be hundreds or even thousands of times higher than the natural background extinction rate, a stark indicator of the severity of the biodiversity crisis. Conservation biology is a critical field dedicated to understanding and mitigating the effects of human activities on biodiversity. Conservation strategies involve protecting habitats, managing populations, restoring degraded ecosystems, and promoting sustainable use of resources.

In conclusion, the evolution of life on Earth is a continuous process shaped by the interplay between organisms and their environment. Natural selection has driven the remarkable diversity of species, giving rise to the intricate ecosystems that support life on our planet. However, the impact of human activities on biodiversity is a serious concern, emphasizing the need for effective conservation measures to safeguard this precious legacy for future generations.

Understanding the principles of evolution, the complexities of ecosystems, and the pervasive influence of human actions on our planet's biodiversity is paramount to securing a sustainable future. The future of life on Earth hinges upon our collective ability to recognize and address these challenges effectively.

The Moons Formation and Geological History

Our journey through the Earth's dynamic history now takes us beyond our planet, to its celestial companion: the Moon. While seemingly barren and unchanging, the Moon holds a rich and complex history, intricately woven with that of Earth itself. Understanding the Moon's formation and geological evolution provides crucial insights not only into our own planet's past but also into the broader processes that have shaped planetary systems throughout the universe.

The most widely accepted theory regarding the Moon's origin is the giant-impact hypothesis. This theory proposes that the Moon formed from debris ejected after a catastrophic collision between the early Earth and a Mars- sized object, often referred to as Theia. This impact, a truly cataclysmic event, occurred billions of years ago, during the tumultuous early stages of our solar system's formation. The sheer force of the collision would have vaporized vast quantities of rock and molten material from both Earth and Theia, creating a swirling disk of debris orbiting the young Earth. Over time, this debris gradually coalesced through a process of accretion, accumulating to form the Moon we see today.

Evidence supporting the giant-impact hypothesis comes from several lines of research. Firstly, the Moon's composition is surprisingly similar to Earth's mantle, suggesting a common origin from Earth's interior. However, the Moon is depleted in volatile elements, elements that readily evaporate at high temperatures, which is consistent with the high temperatures generated during the impact.

Isotopic analysis, a technique that examines the ratios of different isotopes of elements, also supports this hypothesis.

While the exact isotopic signature is a subject of ongoing debate and refinement, the overall data aligns well with a scenario where a significant portion of the Moon's material originated from Earth's mantle. Furthermore, computer simulations of giant impacts have successfully reproduced many of the Moon's observed characteristics, including its orbit, size, and composition.

The Moon's surface, a testament to its geological history, is a landscape of contrasts. The most striking features are the numerous impact craters, which are a ubiquitous record of countless collisions with asteroids and comets throughout its history. The size and distribution of these craters provide invaluable information about the frequency and intensity of impacts over time. Early in its history, the Moon experienced a period of intense bombardment, as evidenced by the heavily cratered highlands. These highlands, the oldest parts of the lunar surface, are composed primarily of anorthosite, a light-colored igneous rock rich in plagioclase feldspar. The formation of these highlands likely involved the solidification of a global magma ocean, a vast sea of molten rock that covered the Moon's surface soon after its formation. As this magma ocean cooled, denser minerals sank towards the interior, while less dense minerals, such as plagioclase feldspar, floated to the surface, forming the anorthosite crust of the highlands.

In contrast to the highlands, the lunar maria, or "seas," are vast, dark, relatively smooth plains primarily composed of basalt. The maria are considerably younger than the highlands and represent extensive volcanic activity that occurred later in the Moon's history. The impact events that created the large basins, later filled with lava, were pivotal in shaping the Moon's landscape. These basins, formed by the force of giant impacts, allowed basaltic lava to well up from the Moon's interior, filling in the depressions and creating the relatively smooth surfaces characteristic of the maria. The ages of the maria, determined using radiometric dating techniques on samples returned by the Apollo missions, indicate that much of the volcanic activity ceased billions of years ago.

The processes that led to the formation of the maria provide essential clues about the Moon's internal structure and thermal evolution. The existence of these extensive basalt flows suggests the Moon once possessed a significant amount of internal heat, allowing for the partial melting of the mantle and the subsequent eruption of lava onto the surface. The Moon's internal heat was likely a consequence of radioactive decay of isotopes like uranium and thorium within its interior, as well as the heat left over from its formation. However, unlike the Earth, the Moon's smaller size and lack of plate tectonics meant that this heat was not effectively dissipated, resulting in volcanism largely confined to specific areas and periods.

The Moon's geological history has not been solely defined by impact events and volcanism. Smaller-scale geological processes have also played a role in shaping its surface.

These include landslides, which have reshaped crater walls and slopes; the formation of rilles, long, narrow channels that might be collapsed lava tubes or tectonic features; and the development of wrinkle ridges, which are probably related to the contraction of the lunar crust as it cooled.

Furthermore, the continuous bombardment by micrometeoroids, although subtle, has gradually modified the lunar regolith, the layer of loose, unconsolidated material that covers the lunar surface. This layer is continuously being churned and mixed by impacts, creating a unique and complex surface layer that is fundamentally different from the underlying bedrock.

The exploration of the Moon, from the first telescopic observations to the Apollo missions and beyond, has revealed a wealth of information about its formation and evolution. The Apollo missions, for instance, brought back samples of lunar rocks that have been subjected to extensive analysis, providing precise ages for different lunar formations and revealing the composition of the lunar crust and mantle. This information has been invaluable in testing and refining our understanding of the Moon's origin and geological history. Modern missions such as the Lunar Reconnaissance Orbiter (LRO) and the Chandrayaan series of missions continue to provide detailed information about the Moon's surface features and internal structure, contributing to our ever-evolving understanding of our closest celestial neighbor.

The Moon's history is therefore not merely a chronicle of impacts and volcanic activity; it is a dynamic interplay of processes, each leaving its distinct imprint on the lunar surface. By studying these features, scientists can piece together a detailed picture of the Moon's evolution, gaining insights into the processes that have shaped planetary bodies throughout the solar system and beyond. The continued exploration and study of the Moon promise to unlock further secrets, enriching our understanding of the processes that created and shaped our planetary system. Moreover, the Moon serves as a valuable testing ground for theories about the formation and evolution of other planetary bodies, extending our knowledge far beyond our own immediate celestial neighborhood. The story of the Moon is therefore intimately intertwined with the larger narrative of the solar system's birth and evolution, making it a fundamental component of our understanding of the cosmos.

Lunar Missions and Discoveries

Our understanding of the Moon has been revolutionized by direct exploration, a journey that began long before the first human set foot on its surface. Early telescopic observations, pioneered by Galileo Galilei and others in the 17th century, provided the first glimpses of the Moon's varied topography – the stark contrast between the heavily cratered highlands and the smoother, darker maria. These initial observations laid the groundwork for future investigations, sparking curiosity and fueling the desire to understand our celestial neighbor.

The limitations of ground-based telescopes, however, restricted the detail that could be gleaned about the Moon's surface. The advent of space exploration in the mid-20th century opened up entirely new possibilities. The Soviet Union took the lead in the early stages of lunar exploration, launching probes like Luna 2, which achieved the first impact on the Moon in 1959, and Luna 9, which successfully performed the first soft landing in 1966, returning the first images from the lunar surface. These missions demonstrated the feasibility of reaching the Moon and gathering data directly from its surface, paving the way for more ambitious endeavors.

The United States' Apollo program, however, stands as a monumental achievement in lunar exploration. Between 1969 and 1972, a series of crewed missions landed twelve astronauts on the Moon. These missions were not merely feats of engineering; they were scientific expeditions of unprecedented scale. The astronauts deployed instruments, conducted experiments, and most importantly, collected a treasure trove of lunar samples. These samples, weighing hundreds of kilograms, provided invaluable data about the Moon's composition, age, and geological history.

The Apollo missions profoundly reshaped our understanding of the Moon. The samples collected revealed the Moon's surprisingly diverse mineralogy. Rocks brought back from the Moon included basalts, anorthosites, and breccias – a testament to the complex geological processes that have shaped its surface. Detailed analysis of these samples provided precise ages for different lunar formations, allowing scientists to reconstruct a chronological sequence of events in the Moon's history. Radiometric dating techniques, based on the decay of radioactive isotopes within the rocks, revealed that the Moon's oldest crustal rocks are over 4 billion years old, offering a glimpse into the early history of our solar system.

Moreover, the Apollo missions provided crucial insights into the Moon's internal structure. Seismic data collected by the Apollo missions revealed that the Moon possesses a relatively small, partially molten core, a solid mantle, and a differentiated crust, which is significantly different than Earth's structure. The discovery of lunar seismic events, some related to meteorite impacts and others seemingly internal in origin, significantly enhanced our knowledge of its geological activity, or lack thereof, over time. This information significantly advanced models of the Moon's thermal evolution and helped constrain theories about its formation. Further understanding was gained by analyzing the composition and age of the lunar samples which showed that the Moon, despite its similarities to Earth, is significantly depleted in volatile elements such as water, further supporting the giant-impact hypothesis of its formation.

The Apollo missions were not only about collecting samples; they also involved a range of scientific experiments conducted on the lunar surface. These included the deployment of seismometers to study lunar quakes, heat- flow probes to measure the Moon's internal temperature, and magnetometers to investigate its magnetic field. These experiments provided crucial data that helped us understand the Moon's internal dynamics and its geological evolution.

The results significantly deepened our appreciation of the processes that have shaped not just the Moon but the formation and evolution of other rocky bodies in the Solar system.

The Apollo legacy continues to inspire exploration and research. Scientists are still meticulously analyzing the lunar samples brought back by the Apollo missions, and new discoveries continue to emerge. Advanced analytical techniques, developed since the Apollo era, allow researchers to extract even finer details about the samples' composition and history. The long-term value of the samples is remarkable and will continue to yield significant discoveries for years to come.

Following the Apollo era, robotic missions continued to explore the Moon, albeit at a reduced pace. However, the late 20th and early 21st centuries saw the commencement of several robotic missions, providing renewed insights into our nearest celestial neighbor. The Clementine mission (1994) and Lunar Prospector (1998) both provided valuable data on the Moon's composition and surface features, providing a more comprehensive, global picture than had previously been available. Clementine, for example, conducted extensive mapping of the lunar surface, revealing unexpected evidence of water ice at the lunar poles. Lunar Prospector, using neutron spectroscopy, detected significant amounts of hydrogen at the poles, strongly supporting the hypothesis of water ice deposits. This discovery has important implications for future human exploration, potentially providing a source of water for life support and rocket propellant.

More recently, missions like the Lunar Reconnaissance Orbiter (LRO) and the Chandrayaan series of missions have revolutionized lunar mapping, providing unprecedented detail on the Moon's surface morphology, composition and geology. LRO has created extremely high-resolution images of the Moon's surface, revealing fascinating features in exquisite detail. These images have been invaluable in studying impact craters, volcanic features, and other geological formations, leading to refined models of the Moon's history. Chandrayaan-1, India's first lunar mission, made significant contributions, including the discovery of water molecules on the lunar surface, corroborating the discoveries of earlier missions.

The continued exploration of the Moon is not only driven by scientific curiosity but also by strategic considerations. The Moon's resources, including water ice and helium-3 (a potential fusion fuel), could play a vital role in future space exploration. Establishing a permanent presence on the Moon, a significant goal for many space agencies, may require utilizing these resources in-situ to reduce the reliance on Earth for materials and resources. Furthermore, the Moon's low gravity and relative proximity to Earth make it an ideal testing ground for technologies and techniques relevant to future missions to Mars and beyond.

The scientific discoveries from lunar missions have also profoundly influenced our understanding of planetary formation and evolution. The Moon serves as a valuable benchmark for testing theories about the formation of other terrestrial planets. The knowledge gained from studying the

Moon, therefore, provides essential context for understanding the broader context of our solar system and planetary systems elsewhere in the universe. The Moon's geological history, recorded in its rocks and surface features, reveals the intensity of early bombardment in the inner solar system. It also speaks to the processes of differentiation, volcanism, and the complex interplay between internal and external forces that shape the surfaces of rocky planets.

In conclusion, the exploration of the Moon, from early telescopic observations to the latest robotic missions, has provided a wealth of information about its formation, evolution, and composition. This knowledge has not only enriched our understanding of our celestial neighbor but has also had far-reaching implications for our understanding of planetary science, the history of our solar system and the possibilities of future space exploration. The Moon continues to hold significant scientific value, acting as a stepping stone for future deep space exploration and offering a wealth of knowledge about the formation and evolution of our solar system and planetary systems in general. The ongoing exploration and analysis of lunar data promise further revelations, enhancing our comprehension of the cosmos and the role of the Moon within the grand narrative of the universe.

The Moons Surface and its Features

The Moon's surface, revealed in breathtaking detail through decades of observation and exploration, presents a captivating tapestry of geological features. Far from being a smooth, uniform sphere, the lunar landscape is a dynamic record of billions of years of cosmic bombardment, volcanic activity, and tectonic processes. This intricate surface, a testament to the violent early history of our solar system, offers invaluable clues to understanding planetary formation and evolution.

The most striking features dominating the lunar landscape are the impact craters, a consequence of countless collisions with asteroids and comets throughout its history. These craters vary enormously in size, from microscopic pits to vast, multi-ringed basins hundreds of kilometers across. The largest impact basins, such as the Imbrium, Serenitatis, and Crisium basins, are immense circular depressions, many of which are filled with the dark, basaltic lava flows known as maria. The formation of these basins involved cataclysmic events that profoundly altered the lunar surface. The impact energy was sufficient to melt vast quantities of lunar rock, creating magma seas that later cooled and solidified, forming the dark plains that are characteristic of the near side of the Moon. The size and distribution of these impact basins offer insights into the intensity and frequency of asteroid bombardment during the early stages of the solar system's formation, a period known as the Late Heavy Bombardment. Analyzing the distribution of craters also helps us to understand the processes of erosion and resurfacing on the Moon, revealing regions that have experienced more recent activity compared to others heavily marked by ancient impacts. The study of impact craters, their size-frequency distribution, and their morphology, is therefore critical to understanding the Moon's impact history and its implications for the wider solar system.

Beyond the impact craters, the lunar surface is marked by a diversity of other landforms. Rugged mountain ranges, remnants of ancient impact events or uplifts caused by internal geological forces, rise dramatically from the lunar plains. These mountains, often found at the rims of large impact basins, are composed predominantly of anorthositic rocks, representing the early, lighter-colored crust of the Moon. The sheer scale of these mountains, some exceeding several kilometers in height, underscores the power of the impacts that created them. These highlands are far older than the maria, their surfaces heavily cratered and exhibiting a complex history of multiple impacts. The contrast between the heavily cratered highlands and the relatively smoother maria provides a visual representation of the different epochs in lunar geological history. The topography of these mountains, particularly their slopes and morphology, provides critical insights into the impact processes that formed them and the subsequent geological processes that have shaped them over time.

Complementing the mountains and craters are the vast expanses of maria, which are low-lying plains of solidified basaltic lava. These dark regions, predominantly located on the near side of the Moon, are relatively young compared to the highlands, formed by volcanic eruptions that occurred billions of years ago. The maria are not perfectly smooth; they are marked by subtle ridges, wrinkles, and domes, reflecting the complexities of the lava flows and subsequent geological processes. The abundance of maria on the near side, compared to the far side, remains a subject of active research, with hypotheses ranging from variations in crustal thickness to the influence of tidal forces on magma distribution. The composition of the maria, as determined by remote sensing and sample analysis, reveals details about the lunar mantle and the processes of magma generation and eruption. The study of the maria, therefore, gives crucial insights into the Moon's volcanic history and the conditions that prevailed in its interior during this period.

The lunar valleys, often referred to as rilles, are long, narrow depressions that cut across the lunar surface. Some rilles are believed to be collapsed lava tubes, channels that once carried molten lava during volcanic eruptions, while others may represent tectonic features created by faulting or other internal processes. The detailed study of these rilles, their morphology, and their association with other geological features helps to improve our understanding of the processes that shaped the lunar surface. Their linear nature often reflects the underlying structures and stress fields within the Moon's crust. Some rilles are associated with specific impact basins, indicating a possible link between the impact event and subsequent lava flows. Others appear to be independent features, highlighting the complexities of the lunar geological history.

A significant difference exists between the near and far sides of the Moon. The near side, the side perpetually facing Earth, is characterized by the extensive maria, while the far side is predominantly covered by the ancient, heavily cratered highlands. This difference in surface features has long intrigued scientists and sparked numerous hypotheses. The leading theories suggest that the thickness of the lunar crust may be a significant contributing factor, with the thinner crust on the near side allowing for more extensive volcanic activity. Another factor may be the influence of tidal forces exerted by Earth, which could have affected the distribution of heat and magma within the lunar interior. The exploration of the far side, through robotic missions, has revealed a fascinating landscape of ancient craters, vast basins, and unique geological formations. This exploration has dramatically improved our understanding of the lunar surface, challenging previous assumptions and leading to new research avenues. High-resolution images obtained by spacecraft like the Lunar Reconnaissance Orbiter have shown previously unknown details of the far side's geology.

The study of the Moon's surface is not limited to visual observation and mapping. Detailed chemical analysis, derived from remote sensing data and lunar samples collected by the Apollo missions, has revealed significant variations in the Moon's composition across different regions. For example, the highlands are primarily composed of anorthosites, a type of feldspar-rich rock, reflecting the early crystallization of the lunar magma ocean. The maria, in contrast, are predominantly composed of basalts, indicative of later volcanic activity. These compositional differences provide crucial insights into the formation and evolution of the Moon and its internal structure. Isotopic analyses of lunar samples reveal details about the origin and history of the lunar material, supporting models of the Moon's formation through a giant impact event. The chemical composition of the lunar rocks and regolith (the layer of dust and fragmented rock on the surface) also provides valuable clues about the early solar system environment.

The continuing exploration of the Moon, through both robotic missions and planned human return missions, promises to significantly advance our knowledge of our closest celestial neighbor. High-resolution imaging, sophisticated spectroscopic analysis, and further sample returns will reveal even finer details about the Moon's surface and geological history. This knowledge will not only enhance our understanding of the Moon's unique evolution but also provide essential context for comprehending the formation and evolution of other terrestrial planets within our solar system and beyond. The Moon, therefore, remains a treasure trove of scientific information, its surface acting as a captivating window into the early history of our solar system and the processes that have shaped the rocky planets we know today. The ongoing analysis of lunar data and future exploration will undoubtedly reveal even more surprising discoveries, further refining our understanding of the Moon's past and enriching our knowledge of the universe. The detailed study of its surface, a record etched in craters, mountains, valleys, and plains, will continue to inspire and challenge us, revealing the intricate story of our celestial companion and its place in the cosmic narrative.

The Moons Influence on Earth Tides and Eclipses

The Moon's gravitational pull, though seemingly subtle from our terrestrial perspective, exerts a profound influence on our planet, manifesting most dramatically in the rhythmic rise and fall of ocean tides and the spectacular celestial events known as eclipses. Understanding these phenomena provides a deeper appreciation for the intricate interplay of gravitational forces within our solar system.

Let's begin with tides, a daily spectacle shaped by the Moon's gravitational tug. The Moon's gravity doesn't simply pull on the Earth as a whole; it pulls more strongly on the side of the Earth facing the Moon, and less strongly on the opposite side. This differential gravitational force stretches the Earth slightly, causing a bulge of water to form on the side facing the Moon – the high tide. Simultaneously, a second bulge forms on the opposite side of the Earth. This seemingly counterintuitive second bulge arises because the Earth, as a whole, is accelerating slightly towards the Moon. The inertia of the water, however, causes it to lag slightly behind, creating a bulge on the far side.

The magnitude of the tidal bulge isn't uniform across the globe. Coastal geography plays a crucial role, with narrow bays and inlets experiencing higher tidal ranges than open coastlines. The shape of the ocean floor, the presence of continental shelves, and even weather patterns all contribute to the complexity of tidal variations. For instance, a narrow bay can funnel the tidal bulge, leading to significantly amplified high tides, while a wide, shallow continental shelf can damp the tidal effect, resulting in lower tidal ranges.

This geographical variability makes tidal prediction a complex science, requiring sophisticated models that incorporate numerous factors. In some regions, the difference between high and low tide can reach staggering heights, exceeding ten meters in extreme cases, such as the Bay of Fundy in Canada. Understanding these local variations is critical for navigation, coastal engineering, and marine biology, as tidal currents play a significant role in marine ecosystems and coastal processes.

Furthermore, the Sun also plays a role in Earth's tides, although its effect is significantly smaller than that of the Moon. The Sun's gravity, despite its immense size, exerts a weaker influence on Earth's tides because of its much greater distance. However, when the Sun, Earth, and Moon align, as during new and full moons, their gravitational forces combine, creating exceptionally high tides known as spring tides. Conversely, when the Sun and Moon are at right angles to each other (during first and third quarter moons), their gravitational forces partially cancel each other out, leading to smaller tidal ranges called neap tides. This cyclical variation in tidal range underscores the complex interplay between the gravitational forces of the Sun and the Moon.

The predictive power of tidal models is crucial for a variety of applications. From predicting the optimal time for launching ships and coastal construction projects, to aiding marine navigation and fisheries management, an accurate understanding of tidal patterns is essential. The development of sophisticated hydrodynamic models, incorporating complex geophysical data, allows scientists to generate increasingly accurate tidal predictions for specific locations. These models take into account numerous factors, including the gravitational forces of the Sun and Moon, the Earth's rotation, ocean bathymetry (the shape of the ocean floor), and even the influence of atmospheric pressure. The accuracy of these predictions is vital for many aspects of human activity, especially in coastal communities, where the constant rhythm of the tides dictates the daily lives of millions.

Beyond tides, the Moon's gravitational influence is powerfully demonstrated during eclipses – breathtaking celestial events that occur when the Sun, Earth, and Moon align in a precise geometric arrangement. There are two types of eclipses: solar and lunar. A solar eclipse occurs when the Moon passes between the Sun and the Earth, casting a shadow on a portion of the Earth's surface. The type of solar eclipse – partial, annular, or total – depends on the relative positions of the Sun, Moon, and Earth. A total solar eclipse, the most spectacular type, occurs when the Moon completely blocks the Sun's disk, revealing the Sun's corona – its outer atmosphere – in a breathtaking display.

The path of totality, the area on Earth where the total eclipse can be observed, is a relatively narrow band that sweeps across the Earth's surface.

The geometry of solar eclipses is critically dependent on the relative distances of the Sun and Moon from the Earth. The Moon's orbit around the Earth is slightly elliptical, meaning its distance from Earth varies over time. This variation in distance influences the apparent size of the Moon in the sky. When the Moon is closer to Earth and its apparent size is larger than the Sun's, it can completely block the Sun's disk, resulting in a total solar eclipse. If the Moon is farther away and its apparent size is smaller, it cannot completely block the Sun, resulting in an annular eclipse, where a bright ring of the Sun remains visible around the Moon's silhouette.

Partial solar eclipses occur when only a portion of the Sun is obscured by the Moon. The precise geometry required for a solar eclipse, a direct alignment of the Sun, Moon, and Earth, is a relatively rare event.

Lunar eclipses, on the other hand, occur when the Earth passes between the Sun and the Moon, casting its shadow on the Moon. Unlike solar eclipses, lunar eclipses are visible from a much wider area of the Earth's surface. During a total lunar eclipse, the Moon passes entirely into the Earth's umbra, the darkest part of its shadow, and takes on a reddish hue, often referred to as a "blood moon." This reddish color is caused by the scattering of sunlight in Earth's atmosphere, which bends some of the red wavelengths of light into the umbra. Partial lunar eclipses occur when only a portion of the Moon passes into the Earth's umbra, while penumbral lunar eclipses involve the Moon passing through the Earth's penumbra, the outer, fainter part of its shadow. The dramatic variations in the Moon's appearance during a lunar eclipse are a compelling demonstration of the interplay of light, shadows, and the geometry of celestial bodies.

The prediction of eclipses is a testament to the precision of our understanding of celestial mechanics. By carefully tracking the positions of the Sun, Earth, and Moon, astronomers can accurately predict the occurrence, type, and visibility of both solar and lunar eclipses years in advance.

These predictions are based on the meticulous application of Kepler's laws of planetary motion and Newton's law of universal gravitation. The accuracy of these predictions highlights the power of scientific modeling in understanding and predicting complex celestial phenomena.

Both tides and eclipses are tangible manifestations of the Moon's gravitational influence on Earth. They are powerful reminders of the dynamic forces that shape our planet and our place in the vast cosmos. The study of these phenomena, from the subtle rhythmic ebb and flow of the tides to the dramatic spectacle of an eclipse, offers a profound insight into the intricate dance of celestial bodies and the profound influence that our celestial neighbor exerts on our planet.

The continued observation and analysis of these phenomena continue to refine our understanding of gravitational forces and the complexities of the solar system. Future research, using increasingly sophisticated observational techniques and modeling capabilities, will further enhance our comprehension of these remarkable displays of celestial mechanics.

Future Exploration of the Moon

The Moon, once the exclusive domain of fleeting visits by robotic probes and a handful of human astronauts, is poised to become a vibrant hub of human activity in the coming decades. Driven by a renewed sense of ambition in space exploration, coupled with technological advancements that were only dreams a few short years ago, plans for a sustained lunar presence are rapidly evolving from aspirational blueprints to concrete projects. These ambitious plans encompass a multitude of objectives, ranging from establishing permanent lunar bases to exploiting the Moon's resources and leveraging its unique location as a springboard for deeper voyages into the solar system.

One of the most prominent goals of future lunar exploration is the establishment of permanent lunar bases. These bases, far from being mere outposts, are envisioned as self- sustaining habitats capable of supporting a sizable crew of scientists, engineers, and other specialists for extended periods. The design and construction of these bases present immense engineering challenges. The harsh lunar environment, characterized by extreme temperature fluctuations, a lack of atmosphere, and constant bombardment by micrometeoroids, necessitates the development of innovative materials and construction techniques. Concepts currently under consideration include utilizing lunar regolith – the Moon's dusty surface layer – as a primary construction material, 3D-printing structures directly from this material, and employing advanced radiation shielding technologies to protect inhabitants from harmful solar and cosmic radiation. The development of closed-loop life support systems, capable of recycling air, water, and waste, is also crucial for ensuring the long-term sustainability of these bases. Power generation will likely involve a combination of solar panels, nuclear fission reactors, or perhaps even innovative solutions utilizing solar energy concentrated by mirrors.

Beyond providing habitable environments, these lunar bases will serve as crucial platforms for scientific research. The Moon's geological record, largely untouched by the processes of plate tectonics and erosion that have reshaped Earth's surface, offers a unique window into the early history of the solar system. Detailed studies of lunar rocks and soil can yield invaluable insights into the formation and evolution of our planetary system, providing clues about the conditions that led to the emergence of life on Earth.

Furthermore, the Moon's lack of atmosphere and magnetic field provides an ideal environment for astronomical observations, free from the interference of terrestrial light pollution and atmospheric distortion. Lunar observatories, shielded from Earth's radio noise, could revolutionize our understanding of the cosmos, enabling the detection of faint signals from distant galaxies and the study of phenomena that are impossible to observe from Earth. The relatively low gravity of the Moon also presents opportunities for unique experiments in physics and materials science, potentially leading to breakthroughs that would be unattainable in Earth's stronger gravitational field.

Another pivotal aspect of future lunar exploration is the extraction and utilization of lunar resources. The Moon is rich in various elements and minerals, including helium-3, a potential fuel for future fusion reactors; water ice, which could be used for drinking water, oxygen production, and rocket propellant; and various metals and minerals vital for construction and manufacturing. The development of efficient techniques for extracting and processing these resources is crucial for making lunar bases truly self-sufficient and reducing the reliance on costly and time- consuming resupply missions from Earth. This will involve significant advancements in robotics, automation, and in-situ resource utilization (ISRU) technologies. ISRU is particularly crucial for reducing the launch mass from Earth, as transporting materials from our planet to the Moon is both energy-intensive and costly. The ability to extract and process resources on the Moon will be a critical factor in making long-term lunar habitation economically and logistically feasible.

The potential economic benefits of lunar resource utilization extend far beyond supporting lunar bases. The extraction of helium-3, for instance, could revolutionize energy production on Earth, providing a clean and potentially limitless energy source. The production of lunar oxygen and water could potentially provide a more accessible supply for use in both terrestrial and extra-terrestrial applications. Rare earth elements and other valuable materials mined on the Moon could also impact the global market, reducing reliance on terrestrial mining operations and potentially leading to more sustainable resource management practices. However, careful consideration must be given to ethical and environmental concerns related to lunar mining, ensuring sustainability and preventing damage to the unique lunar environment.

Finally, the Moon holds significant strategic importance as a potential stepping stone for further space exploration. Its relatively close proximity to Earth makes it an ideal location to test new technologies and refine techniques for long- duration space travel before embarking on more ambitious missions to Mars and beyond. Lunar bases could serve as staging areas for launching missions deeper into the solar system, reducing travel time and fuel requirements. A lunar infrastructure, including fuel depots and habitats, could prove crucial for supporting future human missions to Mars and other celestial bodies. The lower gravity of the Moon compared to Earth also offers advantages for launching spacecraft, reducing the required energy and thus cost of reaching other destinations within our solar system.

The future of lunar exploration is brimming with both promise and challenges. The establishment of permanent lunar bases, the extraction and utilization of lunar resources, and the use of the Moon as a launchpad for deeper space missions represent a paradigm shift in human activity beyond Earth. These endeavors will require significant advancements in various fields, from materials science and robotics to space propulsion and life support technologies.

However, the potential rewards are immense, encompassing not only a deepened understanding of the cosmos and our place within it but also potentially revolutionary advancements in energy production, resource management, and human civilization's reach across the vast expanse of space. The challenges are daunting, but the vision of a sustained human presence on the Moon represents a bold leap forward in humanity's ongoing exploration of the universe, a testament to our enduring curiosity and relentless pursuit of knowledge. The international collaboration necessary to achieve these goals will foster a shared understanding of our shared heritage within our solar system, potentially leading to further cooperation across nations on Earth. The scientific advancements spurred by the ambitions of lunar exploration will not only enrich our understanding of the universe but also provide unforeseen benefits that enhance life and technological possibilities on our own planet. The journey to the Moon, once a symbol of national ambition, is becoming a testament to the collaborative spirit of humanity, a testament to our shared journey into the cosmos.

Mars Atmosphere and Climate

Mars, the fourth planet from the Sun, is a world of stark contrasts, a rusty-red desert planet that holds tantalizing clues to a potentially wetter, warmer past. Understanding Mars' current atmosphere and its dramatic climatic history is crucial to unraveling the mysteries of this fascinating world, and potentially unlocking the secrets of whether life ever existed, or perhaps even still exists, on the Red Planet.

The most striking difference between Mars and Earth is the dramatic disparity in their atmospheric pressures. Earth boasts a robust atmosphere, with an average surface pressure of approximately 1013 millibars, a pressure that sustains liquid water and supports the complex biosphere we know.

Mars, on the other hand, possesses an incredibly thin atmosphere, with a surface pressure averaging a mere 6 millibars—less than 1% of Earth's. This tenuous atmosphere is composed primarily of carbon dioxide (CO_2), making up about 95% of its composition. The remaining 5% is a trace mixture of nitrogen, argon, and other gases, with only minuscule amounts of oxygen and water vapor. This sparse atmosphere offers virtually no protection from the harsh solar radiation and cosmic rays that constantly bombard the Martian surface, a stark contrast to the protective blanket provided by Earth's much denser atmosphere.

The thinness of Mars' atmosphere is directly linked to its low surface gravity. With only about 38% of Earth's gravity, Mars has struggled to retain its atmospheric gases over the vast expanse of geological time. Solar wind, a continuous stream of charged particles emanating from the Sun, has effectively stripped away a significant portion of Mars' atmosphere over billions of years, a process that continues to this day. The lack of a global magnetic field, unlike Earth's protective magnetosphere, further exacerbates this atmospheric erosion, leaving Mars vulnerable to the relentless onslaught of the solar wind.

The absence of a significant magnetic field is another key factor contributing to Mars' current state. Earth's magnetic field acts as a shield, deflecting much of the solar wind and protecting the atmosphere from being stripped away. Mars, however, lost its global magnetic field billions of years ago, a loss that is believed to have been a pivotal moment in the planet's climatic history, ushering in an era of dramatic atmospheric loss and a transition to the cold, dry desert world we observe today. The exact mechanisms behind this loss of the magnetic field remain a subject of ongoing research, with several hypotheses, including changes in the planet's core dynamics, being explored.

Despite its current aridity, evidence strongly suggests that Mars possessed a much denser and warmer atmosphere in its early history, potentially capable of supporting liquid water on its surface. This evidence comes from a variety of sources, including observations from orbiting spacecraft and rovers exploring the Martian surface. Images from orbiting satellites reveal features that strongly resemble ancient riverbeds, lake basins, and even ocean-like formations, hinting at a past where liquid water flowed freely across the Martian landscape. Furthermore, spectroscopic analyses of Martian rocks and soils have revealed the presence of hydrated minerals—minerals that incorporate water molecules into their crystalline structures—providing further confirmation of past aqueous activity.

The rovers exploring the Martian surface have provided even more compelling evidence. The Curiosity rover, for instance, has detected sedimentary rocks that formed in the presence of water, indicating past fluvial or lacustrine environments. The presence of organic molecules, the building blocks of life as we know it, has also been detected in some Martian samples, although their origin remains a subject of ongoing investigation and debate. These findings suggest that Mars may have once harbored a habitable environment, capable of supporting microbial life, raising the tantalizing possibility that life may have once flourished on the Red Planet.

The climatic history of Mars is complex and not fully understood. Scientists believe that early Mars was much warmer and wetter than it is today, potentially due to a denser atmosphere and a stronger greenhouse effect. The greenhouse effect is the process by which certain atmospheric gases trap heat, warming the planet's surface. On Earth, carbon dioxide and water vapor are the primary greenhouse gases. A denser Martian atmosphere, rich in CO_2, could have produced a significant greenhouse effect, keeping the surface warmer and allowing for liquid water to exist. However, the loss of the magnetic field and subsequent atmospheric escape led to a dramatic reduction in atmospheric pressure and a significant cooling of the planet's surface, initiating a transition to the cold, arid conditions observed today.

The exact timing and mechanisms of this climate change are still being investigated. Some scientists believe that the loss of the Martian magnetic field was the primary driver of this climate change. Others propose that large-scale volcanic eruptions, or impact events, may have played a significant role. Whatever the precise causes, the resulting climatic shift was profound and irreversible, transforming Mars from a potentially habitable world into the cold, desolate planet we see today.

One of the major challenges in understanding Mars' past climate is the limited availability of direct evidence. While rovers and orbiting spacecraft have provided valuable insights, the Martian record is incomplete and often difficult to interpret. The absence of plate tectonics on Mars means that the planet's geological history is less well-preserved than on Earth, where plate movements constantly recycle and reshape the surface. Moreover, the lack of widespread erosion on Mars means that older surfaces are more readily preserved, complicating efforts to reconstruct the planet's climatic evolution.

Despite these challenges, significant progress has been made in unraveling the mysteries of Mars' atmosphere and climate. Ongoing research involving advanced rovers, orbiting satellites, and sophisticated climate models is continually refining our understanding of this fascinating world. The search for evidence of past or present life on Mars continues to be a driving force in planetary exploration, fueling the ambition to one day send humans to the Red Planet to conduct further investigations in person.

The exploration of Mars is not merely an exercise in scientific curiosity. Understanding Mars' climate history and atmospheric dynamics provides invaluable insights into the broader context of planetary evolution, helping us understand how planets form, evolve, and potentially become habitable or uninhabitable. The lessons learned from studying Mars can inform our search for life beyond Earth and enhance our understanding of the conditions necessary for the emergence and sustenance of life throughout the universe. The exploration of the Red Planet, therefore, is a journey of discovery that touches upon fundamental questions about our place in the cosmos and the very nature of life itself, an enduring quest that captivates scientists and space enthusiasts alike. The future holds the promise of even more groundbreaking discoveries, as new missions continue to unveil the secrets held within the rusty sands of Mars. The quest for understanding the Martian climate is not merely a scientific endeavor; it's a journey into the depths of our own planetary past, and a potential window into the future of life beyond Earth.

Mars Geology and Surface Features

Mars' geology is a captivating story etched across its rusty surface, a testament to billions of years of dynamic processes. Unlike Earth, Mars lacks plate tectonics, the process of continental drift that constantly reshapes our planet's surface. This absence means that ancient Martian features are remarkably well-preserved, offering scientists a unique window into the planet's past. The Martian landscape is a patchwork of diverse features, each telling a part of the planet's evolutionary narrative.

One of the most striking geological features is the vast canyon system known as Valles Marineris. Stretching over 4,000 kilometers long and reaching depths of up to 7 kilometers, it dwarfs Earth's Grand Canyon. Its scale suggests a formation mechanism significantly different from the erosional processes that carved the Grand Canyon.

Leading theories suggest Valles Marineris formed through a combination of tectonic stretching and subsequent erosion by wind and possibly water. The canyon's intricate network of fissures, layered rock formations, and evidence of past landslides paint a picture of a complex geological history.

The sheer size of Valles Marineris implies significant tectonic forces at work in Mars' early history, a contrast to the geologically static planet we see today. Detailed studies of the canyon's morphology, mineralogy, and stratigraphy continue to unravel the story of its formation and its role in the planet's evolution.

Then there's Olympus Mons, the largest volcano in our solar system. Towering over 25 kilometers above the surrounding plains, this colossal shield volcano dwarfs even the largest volcanoes on Earth. Its gentle slopes and immense size are indicative of its formation from highly fluid lava flows over an extended period. The lack of plate tectonics on Mars allowed Olympus Mons to remain in one location for millions of years, growing ever larger with each eruption.

The volcano's massive caldera, a depression formed by the collapse of the summit, suggests past cataclysmic eruptions that reshaped the surrounding landscape. The immense size and longevity of Olympus Mons underscores the significant volcanic activity that has shaped the Martian surface. Its flanks are scarred by numerous lava flows, channels, and debris aprons, each a frozen snapshot of past eruptive events. Studying these features helps scientists determine the duration and intensity of volcanic activity, as well as the composition and viscosity of the erupted lava.

Beyond Olympus Mons, Mars boasts a number of other large shield volcanoes, clustered mainly in the Tharsis region.

These volcanoes, though smaller than Olympus Mons, are still impressive in scale. Their collective eruptive history contributed significantly to the planet's atmosphere and surface composition. The volcanic activity on Mars, coupled with evidence of past hydrothermal activity, suggests potential habitats for microbial life in the planet's distant past. The distribution of these volcanoes, clustered together in Tharsis, suggests a relationship between regional tectonic stresses and the concentration of volcanic activity. Analyzing the age and composition of these volcanoes offers critical information about the timing and nature of Mars' volcanic past.

The Martian surface is also heavily scarred by impact craters, a record of past asteroid and comet bombardments. The density and size distribution of these craters provide clues to the age of different Martian terrains. Older surfaces, such as the heavily cratered southern highlands, bear witness to the early heavy bombardment period of the solar system.

The younger northern lowlands, on the other hand, show fewer craters, suggesting that they formed later in Martian history, perhaps through large-scale resurfacing events. The size and distribution of these craters provide insights into the frequency and intensity of past impacts. The study of impact craters, combined with radiometric dating of Martian rocks, allows scientists to construct a detailed chronology of the planet's geological history.

In addition to volcanoes and impact craters, Mars' surface is characterized by extensive systems of channels and valleys, suggesting the past presence of liquid water. Some of these features resemble ancient riverbeds, with intricate branching patterns and erosional features similar to those found on Earth. Other channels suggest catastrophic flooding events, potentially caused by sudden releases of subsurface water.

The detection of hydrated minerals in Martian rocks further supports the hypothesis of past water activity. The presence of these channels and valleys highlights the importance of water in shaping the Martian landscape, hinting at a much wetter past. The exact timing and duration of water flow are still subjects of ongoing research, but the evidence suggests that Mars may have once had a more active hydrological cycle.

Mars' polar ice caps are another captivating feature, consisting primarily of water ice, with a significant amount of frozen carbon dioxide (dry ice) also present. Seasonal variations in the size and composition of these ice caps are significant, reflecting changes in atmospheric pressure and temperature. The layered structure of the ice caps, visible in high-resolution images, reveals a record of past climatic fluctuations. Analyzing these layers offers invaluable insights into the long-term changes in Mars' climate, providing a glimpse into the planet's long-term climatic history.

The potential for subsurface water on Mars is a crucial area of investigation. Evidence from orbiting satellites and rovers points to the possibility of subsurface reservoirs of water ice and even liquid brine. The existence of such subsurface reservoirs could have significant implications for the possibility of past or present life on Mars. The presence of permafrost, or permanently frozen ground, suggests that water could exist in subsurface layers. Radar sounding experiments have detected features consistent with subsurface ice deposits, and the detection of recurring slope lineae (RSL), dark streaks appearing on slopes during warmer seasons, suggests the possibility of liquid water flow. Although the exact nature of RSL remains debated, their existence hints at the presence of liquid water at or near the surface under certain conditions.

The geological history of Mars is a complex interplay of impact cratering, volcanic activity, tectonic processes, and the action of water and wind. Understanding this history requires a multidisciplinary approach, integrating data from orbital observations, rover explorations, and laboratory analyses of Martian meteorites. The challenges are significant, but the potential rewards are immense.

Unraveling the mysteries of Mars' geology holds the key to understanding its climatic evolution, its potential for past habitability, and the broader context of planetary formation and evolution within our solar system and beyond. Further missions and technological advancements promise to yield even more exciting discoveries, bringing us closer to a complete understanding of the Red Planet's geological narrative. The story of Mars is far from over; it is still being written, and we are privileged to be witnesses to this unfolding tale of a world both familiar and alien.

The Search for Life on Mars

The tantalizing possibility of life on Mars has driven exploration for decades, fueling ambitious missions and inspiring countless scientific endeavors. The search isn't simply about finding microscopic organisms; it's about understanding the fundamental principles of life itself, its emergence, its resilience, and its potential to exist beyond Earth. This quest demands a multi-faceted approach, integrating data from orbital observations, robotic exploration, and the analysis of Martian meteorites.

One of the most crucial aspects of the search is the identification of biosignatures – any substance or structure that provides scientific evidence of past or present life.

These biosignatures can take many forms, from fossilized microbial structures to distinctive isotopic ratios in rocks, indicative of biological processes. The challenge lies in distinguishing between biosignatures and abiogenic features, processes that create similar patterns without the involvement of life. This requires sophisticated analytical techniques and a deep understanding of Mars' geological history.

The Viking missions of the 1970s marked a pivotal moment in the search for Martian life. While their experiments yielded ambiguous results, they provided valuable insights into the Martian environment and spurred further investigation. The Viking landers conducted experiments designed to detect metabolic activity in Martian soil samples. Although some initial results hinted at positive findings, these were later attributed to chemical reactions, not biological processes. The Viking missions, though ultimately inconclusive in terms of life detection, significantly advanced our understanding of Martian soil chemistry and laid the foundation for future explorations.

Subsequent missions, such as the Mars Exploration Rovers (Spirit and Opportunity) and the Mars Science Laboratory rover Curiosity, have significantly expanded our knowledge of the Martian environment. These rovers have explored diverse Martian terrains, analyzing rocks and soil for clues to past habitability and potential biosignatures. Spirit and Opportunity, deployed in 2004, discovered evidence of past water activity, including minerals that form in the presence of water. Curiosity, landing in 2012, has found organic molecules – the building blocks of life – in Martian rocks.

While the origin of these molecules remains uncertain – whether they are biological or abiogenic – their presence demonstrates that the Martian environment once possessed the necessary chemical components for life to emerge.

The Perseverance rover, which landed on Mars in 2021, represents a significant leap forward in the search for life. Its primary mission is astrobiology, focused on searching for signs of ancient microbial life and collecting samples for eventual return to Earth. Perseverance is equipped with an advanced suite of scientific instruments, enabling it to analyze Martian rocks and soil with unprecedented detail.

It's carrying a sophisticated instrument called SHERLOC (Scanning Habitable Environments with Raman & Luminescence for Organics & Chemicals), capable of detecting organic molecules and identifying potential biosignatures. This rover also deployed the Ingenuity helicopter, the first aircraft to fly on another planet, expanding exploration capabilities and access to previously unreachable locations.

The ongoing exploration of Mars is not limited to surface missions. Orbiters, such as the Mars Reconnaissance Orbiter

(MRO) and the Trace Gas Orbiter (TGO), play a critical role in identifying promising landing sites and providing global context for surface-based discoveries. MRO has high- resolution cameras and spectrometers, providing detailed images and compositional maps of the Martian surface, helping identify regions of past water activity and potential biosignatures. The TGO focuses on analyzing trace gases in the Martian atmosphere, searching for potential biomarkers that could indicate biological processes.

The analysis of Martian meteorites found on Earth also contributes significantly to the search for life. These meteorites offer a glimpse into the Martian interior and provide samples that can be analyzed in sophisticated Earth- based laboratories. Some Martian meteorites have revealed potential evidence of past microbial life, although the interpretations remain contentious within the scientific community. These findings highlight the importance of continued analysis of Martian meteorites, as they offer a unique perspective on the planet's history and potential for life.

One of the most significant challenges in the search for life on Mars is the possibility of contamination. Earth-based organisms could inadvertently be transported to Mars during missions, potentially obscuring any evidence of indigenous Martian life. This necessitates meticulous sterilization procedures for spacecraft and instruments before they are launched.

Another significant hurdle is the harsh Martian environment. The extreme cold, thin atmosphere, and high levels of radiation pose significant challenges for life. Even if life existed on Mars in the past, it may have left behind only subtle traces that are difficult to detect. This reinforces the need for increasingly sophisticated detection methods and prolonged exploration.

The search for life on Mars is a long-term endeavor requiring international collaboration and technological innovation. Future missions will involve more advanced robotic explorers, potentially including sample-return missions, bringing Martian samples back to Earth for more detailed analysis. These missions will be crucial in definitively answering the long-standing question of whether life ever existed, or perhaps even still exists, on the Red Planet.

The potential discovery of past or present life on Mars would revolutionize our understanding of life's universality and our place in the cosmos. It would not only confirm that life is not unique to Earth, but also provide invaluable insights into the conditions under which life can emerge and evolve. The quest continues, and the possibilities remain breathtaking.

Each new discovery, each new mission, brings us closer to unraveling the mysteries of Mars and the potential for life beyond Earth. The pursuit of understanding the Red Planet's past and present is a testament to humanity's enduring curiosity and our relentless quest to explore the unknown.

The story of Mars, and the search for life within its enigmatic landscape, is a story still unfolding, a narrative written in the dust and rock of a distant world, waiting to be fully deciphered.

Mars Exploration Missions Past Present and Future

The exploration of Mars represents a remarkable chapter in human history, a testament to our enduring curiosity and our relentless pursuit of knowledge. Our journey to the Red Planet began not with daring astronauts, but with robotic emissaries, each mission building upon the successes and failures of its predecessors, steadily refining our understanding of this enigmatic world.

The early missions, largely during the 1960s and 70s, were characterized by a pioneering spirit, often grappling with the technological limitations of the era. The Mariner missions, a series of flybys and orbiters, provided the first close-up images of Mars, revealing a desolate yet intriguing landscape. These missions mapped the planet's surface, providing crucial data for future landing attempts, and uncovered evidence of vast canyons and extinct volcanoes, hinting at a geologically dynamic past. The Mariner 9 orbiter, arriving in 1971, was particularly significant, mapping approximately 85% of the Martian surface before the dust storms subsided, revealing the planet's surprisingly diverse geology.

The Viking program, launched in the mid-1970s, marked a watershed moment. Two landers, Viking 1 and Viking 2, successfully touched down on the Martian surface, carrying instruments designed to search for evidence of life. This represented a giant leap forward in our ambition to understand the possibility of extraterrestrial life. The Viking landers performed a suite of experiments, analyzing Martian soil for signs of biological activity. While these experiments did not definitively confirm the presence of life, they generated considerable excitement and debate within the scientific community. The results, while ambiguous, provided valuable data on Martian soil chemistry and atmospheric composition, laying the foundation for future investigations. The inconclusive nature of the Viking results, however, served as a valuable lesson, highlighting the complexity of detecting life in such an alien environment and emphasizing the need for more sophisticated techniques and approaches.

The long hiatus following the Viking program provided time for technological advancements and the refinement of scientific strategies. The subsequent missions, such as the Mars Pathfinder mission in 1997, marked a renewed push towards Martian exploration. Pathfinder, deploying the Sojourner rover, demonstrated the feasibility of exploring the Martian surface with mobile robotic platforms. Sojourner's relatively short lifespan and limited mobility still provided invaluable insights into the Martian terrain and provided images that significantly enhanced our understanding of the planet's geological composition.

The Mars Exploration Rovers (MER), Spirit and Opportunity, launched in 2003, represent a significant step forward in our exploration of Mars. These rovers far exceeded their planned operational lifetimes, significantly extending our understanding of the planet. Spirit and Opportunity extensively explored the Martian landscape, collecting data on rocks and soil, providing compelling evidence of past water activity. Their discoveries, including the identification of minerals that form in the presence of water, strongly suggested that Mars was once a much warmer and wetter place, perhaps even capable of supporting life. The longevity of these rovers was a testament to the innovative engineering and design of the mission.

The Mars Science Laboratory (MSL) mission, with its rover Curiosity, launched in 2011, represents a new level of sophistication in Martian exploration. Curiosity, a significantly larger and more technologically advanced rover than its predecessors, has been exploring the Gale Crater, a region believed to have once contained a lake. Its advanced scientific instruments allow for detailed analyses of Martian rocks and soil, revealing the presence of organic molecules – the building blocks of life – further fueling the debate about the planet's potential habitability. Curiosity's findings, though not definitive proof of past life, strengthen the case for past habitability and highlight the complexity of the Martian geological history.

The Perseverance rover, which landed in Jezero Crater in 2021, represents the most ambitious Mars mission to date. Its primary goal is astrobiology – searching for signs of ancient microbial life. Perseverance is equipped with a wide array of scientific instruments, including SHERLOC (Scanning Habitable Environments with Raman & Luminescence for Organics & Chemicals), capable of detecting organic molecules and identifying potential biosignatures. It is also collecting samples for eventual return to Earth, a monumental undertaking that will allow scientists to analyze Martian samples with the most advanced laboratory equipment available. The Ingenuity helicopter, deployed by Perseverance, represents a remarkable technological achievement, demonstrating the potential for aerial exploration of the Martian surface, expanding access to previously unreachable terrains.

The exploration of Mars is not solely confined to the surface. Orbiters such as the Mars Reconnaissance Orbiter (MRO) and the Trace Gas Orbiter (TGO) play a crucial role, providing global context for surface-based discoveries.

MRO, with its high-resolution cameras and spectrometers,

has mapped the planet's surface in exquisite detail, identifying potential landing sites and revealing evidence of past water activity. TGO focuses on analyzing trace gases in the Martian atmosphere, searching for potential biomarkers that could indicate biological processes. These orbital missions provide a critical global perspective, complementing the localized explorations conducted by the rovers.

The analysis of Martian meteorites found on Earth further contributes to our understanding of the Red Planet. These meteorites, ejected from Mars by asteroid impacts, provide valuable samples that can be extensively analyzed in Earth- based laboratories. Some Martian meteorites have shown indications of possible past microbial life, further stimulating research and discussions in the scientific community.

However, the interpretation of these findings often remains contentious, requiring rigorous validation and further investigation.

Looking towards the future, ambitious plans are underway for even more sophisticated missions. Sample-return missions, currently in various stages of planning, will bring Martian samples back to Earth for detailed analysis, offering an unparalleled opportunity to answer fundamental questions about the planet's history and the potential for past or present life. These missions will require international collaboration and significant technological advancements, underscoring the global effort involved in unraveling the mysteries of Mars.

The challenges inherent in Martian exploration are significant. The extreme cold, thin atmosphere, and high levels of radiation pose significant hurdles for both robotic missions and, ultimately, human exploration. The meticulous sterilization of spacecraft is crucial to prevent contamination of Mars with terrestrial organisms, ensuring that any potential discovery of Martian life is not compromised by Earth-based contamination.

The search for life on Mars is a long-term endeavor, requiring patience, persistence, and a commitment to scientific rigor. The discoveries made to date have provided tantalizing glimpses into the potential for past habitability, but the definitive answer to the question of whether life existed or exists on Mars remains elusive. The journey, however, is far from over; the relentless pursuit of knowledge drives us onward, towards a future where we may finally unlock the secrets hidden within the red dust of our neighboring planet. The exploration of Mars is a testament to human ingenuity and our unyielding desire to explore the cosmos, a testament to our place in the universe, and a story that continues to unfold with each new discovery.

Colonizing Mars Challenges and Possibilities

The tantalizing prospect of a human colony on Mars, once relegated to the realm of science fiction, is rapidly becoming a tangible goal. However, the journey from scientific exploration to permanent human settlement presents a formidable set of challenges, demanding innovative solutions and a profound understanding of the Martian environment. The harsh realities of the Red Planet—a thin, carbon dioxide-rich atmosphere offering negligible protection from radiation, extreme temperature fluctuations, and a lack of readily available water and nutrients—pose significant hurdles.

One of the most immediate and critical challenges is radiation. Mars lacks a global magnetic field and a thick atmosphere, leaving its surface exposed to high levels of solar and cosmic radiation. This radiation poses a serious health risk to human colonists, increasing the risk of cancer, radiation sickness, and other detrimental health effects.

Shielding colonists from this radiation will require substantial engineering efforts, potentially involving the construction of underground habitats or the development of advanced radiation-resistant materials. This necessitates extensive research into radiation shielding technologies, testing materials that can effectively mitigate the harmful effects of radiation, while keeping the weight and logistics of transportation to Mars in mind. Innovative solutions might involve using Martian regolith (soil) itself as a radiation shield, layering it around habitats to provide natural protection.

The scarcity of readily available resources is another significant obstacle. Water, crucial for human survival, is not readily available on the surface of Mars. While evidence strongly suggests the presence of subsurface ice, accessing and extracting it requires significant technological investment and energy consumption. The extraction process must be efficient and sustainable, considering the constraints of operating on a distant planet. In-situ resource utilization (ISRU) will become critical; this involves using Martian resources to create necessary supplies like oxygen, water, and building materials, significantly reducing the reliance on Earth-based supplies. The production of oxygen from Martian atmospheric CO2, for example, is a crucial area of current research, with various technologies, such as the Mars Oxygen ISRU Experiment (MOXIE) on the Perseverance rover, demonstrating promising results. Similarly, developing methods to extract water ice and potentially using it to grow food would drastically improve the self- sufficiency of a Martian colony.

Temperature extremes represent another considerable challenge. The Martian surface experiences drastic temperature variations, ranging from -125°C (-193°F) at night to a comparatively balmy 20°C (68°F) during the day at the equator. Maintaining a habitable temperature in human settlements will necessitate robust thermal insulation and potentially active climate control systems, relying on efficient and reliable power sources. This requires developing energy-efficient technologies that can withstand the Martian environment and operate consistently. Nuclear power, solar energy, and potentially even wind energy could play vital roles in powering a Mars colony, but each has limitations and challenges in the Martian context that require significant investigation.

The psychological effects of living in a confined environment, isolated from Earth, for extended periods must also be carefully considered. The psychological impact of isolation, confinement, and the inherent risks of living on Mars will require comprehensive countermeasures. A strong emphasis on crew selection, training, and psychological support will be essential to maintain the well-being and productivity of the colony's inhabitants. Virtual reality technology, communication systems with minimal latency, and even planned recreational activities could help mitigate the negative psychological effects of isolation.

Beyond the purely technological and environmental challenges, the ethical considerations are equally important. The prevention of planetary contamination is paramount.

Introducing terrestrial microorganisms to Mars could compromise any potential discovery of indigenous life, potentially irrevocably altering the Martian environment. Strict planetary protection protocols are necessary, requiring rigorous sterilization procedures for all spacecraft and equipment sent to Mars. This includes not just preventing the introduction of Earth-based life but also preventing the accidental return of potentially hazardous Martian organisms to Earth.

Furthermore, the long-term sustainability of a Martian colony will require a sophisticated understanding of the Martian ecosystem, even if that ecosystem is currently largely dormant. Any human activity on Mars must strive to minimize its impact on the planet, to ensure the preservation of its scientific value. This may involve developing technologies that enable the restoration of a more hospitable environment on Mars, potentially through terraforming, a concept fraught with its own ethical implications. Any attempt to alter Mars's environment significantly must be approached cautiously and with a comprehensive understanding of its potential consequences. The ethical considerations surrounding terraforming are significant and deserve extensive debate and careful planning.

Establishing a self-sustaining colony on Mars will not be a single, grand endeavor but rather a gradual process involving iterative steps, starting with incremental expansions of the infrastructure and capabilities of initial outposts. The establishment of a robust supply chain between Earth and Mars, initially relying on frequent resupply missions, will gradually shift towards increased reliance on Martian resources as ISRU technologies mature. This transition requires a long-term commitment to continuous technological development and international collaboration.

The economic aspects of Mars colonization are considerable, demanding substantial investment and potentially a shift towards a global, collaborative approach to fund such an ambitious undertaking. Private sector involvement, alongside government funding, will likely be crucial to achieve the economic scale necessary for sustained colonization.

Moreover, the legal framework for governing a Martian colony and the rights and responsibilities of its inhabitants will need to be established, ensuring a framework that aligns with international law and ethical principles.

The colonization of Mars represents a momentous endeavor, pushing the boundaries of human ingenuity and our capacity for collaboration. The challenges are substantial, but so are the possibilities. The prospect of establishing a self- sustaining human presence on another planet represents a profound step forward in human civilization, offering the opportunity to expand our species' reach and potentially uncover new scientific knowledge that could benefit humankind. The journey to a Martian colony will be a long and challenging one, but the potential rewards, both scientific and existential, make the pursuit more than worthwhile. The future of humanity may well depend on our success in navigating these challenges and realizing the dream of a permanent human presence on the Red Planet.

The Milky Way Galaxy Our Cosmic Home

Our journey through the cosmos continues, having contemplated the challenges and triumphs of potential Martian colonization. Now, let's shift our gaze to a grander scale, to our cosmic home: the Milky Way Galaxy. This immense island of stars, gas, and dust is a breathtaking testament to the power of gravity and the awe-inspiring expanse of the universe. Understanding its structure, contents, and place within the larger cosmological landscape is crucial to grasping our own cosmic significance.

The Milky Way, as seen from Earth on a clear, dark night, appears as a faint, luminous band stretching across the sky. This ethereal glow, known for millennia, is the combined light of billions of stars too distant to be individually resolved by the naked eye. Early astronomers, lacking the technology to unravel its true nature, could only speculate about its composition and extent. Today, however, armed with powerful telescopes and sophisticated instruments, we possess a far more detailed understanding of our galactic home.

The Milky Way is classified as a barred spiral galaxy. This designation reveals key aspects of its structure. The "barred" component refers to a central bar-shaped structure of stars, gas, and dust, extending across the galaxy's core. This bar is not a static feature but rotates, influencing the dynamics of the galaxy as a whole. The "spiral" aspect describes the sweeping arms that emanate from the ends of the bar, spiraling outward like a cosmic pinwheel. These arms are regions of intense star formation, where clouds of gas and dust collapse under their own gravity, igniting the fiery hearts of new stars.

These spiral arms are not solid, rigid structures; rather, they are density waves – regions of enhanced density propagating through the galactic disk. As these waves move, they compress the interstellar medium (the gas and dust between stars), triggering the formation of new stars. This explains why the spiral arms are brighter and more prominent than the regions between them. Stars within these arms often form in clusters, bound together by mutual gravitational attraction. These stellar nurseries showcase the dynamic nature of our galaxy, constantly birthing and evolving.

Observations suggest that these spiral arms are not perfectly symmetrical, exhibiting irregularities and variations in their density and structure. The ongoing gravitational interactions between stars, gas clouds, and dark matter contribute to these dynamic patterns.

Beyond the spiral arms lies the galactic bulge, a dense, spherical region of stars surrounding the galactic center. The bulge is comprised primarily of older, redder stars, indicating a slower rate of star formation compared to the spiral arms.

The stars in the bulge are more densely packed than those in the disk, resulting in a brighter and more concentrated region of light. Astronomers believe the bulge formed early in the Milky Way's history, from the initial collapse of the galactic gas cloud. The complex motions and gravitational interactions within the bulge are still being actively researched, providing insights into the galaxy's early evolution and the distribution of mass within its core.

Enveloping the disk and the bulge is a vast, spherical halo. This halo extends far beyond the visible disk, containing a scattered population of stars, globular clusters (dense, spherical collections of hundreds of thousands of stars), and a significant amount of dark matter. The stars in the halo are generally older than those in the disk, providing further evidence for an evolutionary pathway wherein the halo formed earlier, followed by the disk. Globular clusters, each containing hundreds of thousands of stars all orbiting the galactic center in a synchronized manner, are thought to be some of the oldest objects in the Milky Way, having formed soon after the Big Bang. The halo's dark matter component, which makes up a significant portion of its mass, remains largely mysterious but plays a crucial role in the galaxy's gravitational dynamics.

The Milky Way is a vast collection of various stellar types, their distribution closely tied to the galaxy's structure. In the spiral arms, we find a mixture of young, hot, blue stars and older, cooler, redder stars. However, the concentration of young, massive, blue stars is significantly higher in the spiral arms. These stars have short lifespans, exploding as supernovae and enriching the interstellar medium with heavy elements. The older stars tend to be found throughout the galaxy, with a greater concentration in the galactic bulge and halo. Red giants, evolved stars that have expanded and cooled, are also prevalent in the bulge and halo. These evolved stars provide valuable clues about the age and history of the Milky Way.

White dwarfs, the remnants of low-mass stars, are found scattered throughout the galaxy, their faint glow a testament to their long, cooling lives. Neutron stars, incredibly dense objects formed from the collapsed cores of massive stars, and black holes, regions of spacetime with such intense gravity that not even light can escape, are also present in our galaxy. These compact objects represent the final stages of stellar evolution, some forming through supernova explosions and others through the gradual collapse of massive stars. Their locations and distribution help astronomers understand the evolutionary pathways of stars and their influence on the galactic environment.

The Milky Way's structure and content are not static; they are constantly evolving under the influence of gravity. Stars are born, live, and die, continuously altering the composition and distribution of matter within the galaxy. The spiral arms are dynamic waves of density, constantly changing their shape and position. Collisions with smaller galaxies, a common occurrence in the universe, add new stars and gas to the Milky Way, further altering its structure and dynamics.

Evidence suggests that the Milky Way has cannibalized smaller galaxies in its past, incorporating their stars and gas into its own structure. These galactic mergers play a crucial role in shaping the galaxies we observe today.

The study of the Milky Way involves a variety of observational techniques, encompassing a broad spectrum of electromagnetic radiation. Visible light observations provide information about the distribution of stars and their properties. Infrared observations penetrate the dust clouds that obscure much of the visible light, allowing us to study regions of star formation and the center of the galaxy. Radio observations unveil the presence of neutral hydrogen gas and other molecules in the interstellar medium. X-ray and gamma-ray observations reveal high-energy processes associated with black holes and neutron stars. The combined insights from these different observational windows have created a remarkably detailed picture of our galactic home.

Furthermore, the study of the Milky Way benefits from the application of sophisticated computational models. These models simulate the gravitational interactions between stars, gas, and dark matter, allowing astronomers to predict the galaxy's evolution and compare their predictions with observations. By incorporating data from various observational techniques and refining the models, our understanding of the Milky Way's structure, dynamics, and formation is continuously improving. This collaborative approach, combining theoretical modeling with observational data, is essential to unlocking the secrets of our galactic home.

In conclusion, the Milky Way Galaxy, our cosmic home, is a vast and intricate structure composed of billions of stars, gas, dust, and dark matter. Its spiral arms, central bulge, and encompassing halo represent distinct regions with different stellar populations and evolutionary histories. The continuous birth, life, and death of stars, coupled with the galaxy's dynamic interactions with other galaxies, continually reshape its appearance and character. Through ongoing observations and sophisticated modeling, we steadily increase our understanding of this majestic spiral, gaining crucial insights into the processes that shape galaxies and our place within the cosmos. Our journey into the universe continues, from the challenges of Mars to the breathtaking scale of our own galaxy, demonstrating the ceaseless exploration and understanding that characterize our scientific pursuit of knowledge.

Types of Galaxies Spiral Elliptical and Irregular

Having established a detailed understanding of our own Milky Way galaxy, a barred spiral, it's time to broaden our perspective and explore the incredible diversity of galaxies that populate the observable universe. These celestial islands, each a vast collection of stars, gas, and dark matter, come in a dazzling array of shapes, sizes, and compositions. While the Milky Way serves as a valuable reference point, it represents only one type among a much larger cosmic tapestry.

The most prevalent classification scheme divides galaxies into three primary categories: spiral, elliptical, and irregular. Within each category, further sub-classifications exist, reflecting the subtleties and nuances in galactic structure.

These classifications are not arbitrary but reflect fundamental differences in their formation, evolution, and internal dynamics. Understanding these differences provides crucial insights into the processes that shape galaxies and the universe itself.

Let's begin with spiral galaxies, perhaps the most visually striking type. As their name suggests, these galaxies are characterized by a prominent, flattened disk of stars, gas, and dust, with spiral arms gracefully winding outwards from a central bulge. The Milky Way, as we've seen, is a prime example. The spiral arms are not merely decorative features; they are regions of active star formation, where dense clouds of gas and dust collapse under their own gravity, igniting the birth of new stars. These stellar nurseries are often ablaze with the brilliant light of young, massive, blue stars, which burn brightly but have relatively short lifespans. The contrast between these bright arms and the darker spaces between them creates the characteristic spiral pattern.

The central bulge, a dense, spheroidal concentration of stars, often contains older, redder stars. This indicates a different star formation history compared to the spiral arms. The bulge likely formed early in the galaxy's life, from the initial collapse of the gas cloud that gave rise to the galaxy. Beyond the disk and bulge, many spiral galaxies possess a vast, spherical halo, extending far beyond the visible disk, containing older stars, globular clusters, and a significant fraction of dark matter. The halo's dark matter plays a critical role in the galaxy's overall gravitational structure and stability.

Spiral galaxies are further categorized into different subtypes based on the prominence of their central bulge and the tightness of their spiral arms. For example, Sa galaxies have large bulges and tightly wound spiral arms, while Sc galaxies have smaller bulges and loosely wound arms. Between these extremes lie Sb galaxies, exhibiting intermediate characteristics. The presence or absence of a central bar, as in our Milky Way, is another important distinguishing feature, further refining the classification. These variations reflect the complex interplay of factors during a galaxy's formation and evolution, including the initial gas cloud's properties, the presence of mergers, and the influence of dark matter.

Elliptical galaxies, in contrast to spirals, are characterized by their smooth, ellipsoidal shape and a lack of prominent spiral arms. These galaxies typically contain a large population of older, redder stars, with relatively little gas and dust. This suggests a lower rate of ongoing star formation compared to spiral galaxies. Elliptical galaxies range in size from relatively small dwarf ellipticals to giant elliptical galaxies, among the largest structures in the universe. The size and shape of an elliptical galaxy are believed to be related to its formation history, with larger galaxies often resulting from mergers of smaller galaxies. The lack of gas and dust in many ellipticals implies that most star formation occurred early in their history, leaving behind a population of older stars.

Interestingly, the stars in elliptical galaxies exhibit a random, rather than organized, motion, unlike the more structured rotation observed in spiral galaxies. This chaotic motion may be a consequence of multiple galactic mergers contributing to their formation. The absence of significant gas and dust in many ellipticals also suggests a less dynamic environment, with fewer regions of active star formation. However, some elliptical galaxies do possess some gas and dust, indicating that some level of star formation might still be occurring, though at a significantly lower rate than in spiral galaxies.

The study of elliptical galaxies provides crucial insights into the processes that drive galaxy mergers and the ultimate fate of galaxies.

Irregular galaxies, as their name suggests, lack the well- defined structure of spiral and elliptical galaxies. They are characterized by a chaotic distribution of stars, gas, and dust, with no clear symmetry or organized spiral arms. These galaxies often exhibit intense star formation activity, as evidenced by the presence of numerous young, blue stars.

Many irregular galaxies are thought to be the result of gravitational interactions with other galaxies, leading to a disruption of their initial structure. These interactions can trigger bursts of star formation, leading to the intense activity observed in many irregular galaxies.

Some irregular galaxies are simply small and lack the sufficient mass to develop a well-defined structure. Others might have been originally spiral or elliptical but have been distorted by gravitational encounters. The irregular classification is a catch-all for galaxies that don't neatly fit into the spiral or elliptical categories, highlighting the universe's capacity for diversity. Observational studies reveal that irregular galaxies often show significant amounts of gas and dust, which is crucial for ongoing star formation. These galaxies play a vital role in the recycling of matter in the universe, contributing to the enrichment of the interstellar medium with heavy elements produced by stellar nucleosynthesis.

The study of galaxy types is far from complete. Ongoing research constantly refines our understanding of these celestial structures. New observational techniques, especially in the infrared and radio wavebands, provide deeper insights into the hidden aspects of galaxies. Sophisticated computer simulations also aid in modeling galaxy formation and evolution, allowing researchers to test theories against observations. The diversity of galaxies reflects a complex interplay of factors, from initial conditions to gravitational interactions. These factors contribute to the fascinating tapestry of shapes, sizes, and internal dynamics seen throughout the universe. Our understanding of the cosmic landscape is continually improving as astronomers unravel the intricacies of these island universes, bringing us closer to a comprehensive picture of our universe's history and structure. The quest to understand the universe's diverse population of galaxies continues, driven by the ever- improving observational techniques and theoretical models that are constantly refining our view of the cosmos.

Galaxy Formation and Evolution

The breathtaking diversity of galaxies, as we've explored, extends beyond their simple classification into spirals, ellipticals, and irregulars. To truly grasp the cosmic tapestry, we must delve into the processes that have sculpted these celestial islands over billions of years: galaxy formation and evolution. This journey takes us back to the very dawn of the universe, a time when the seeds of these magnificent structures were sown.

The prevailing cosmological model, the Lambda-CDM model (ΛCDM), provides the framework for understanding galaxy formation. ΛCDM posits that the universe began with a period of rapid expansion known as inflation, followed by a hot, dense state where fundamental particles formed. As the universe cooled and expanded, gravity played a crucial role, pulling together denser regions of matter. These denser regions, initially subtle fluctuations in the early universe's density, became the seeds of future galaxies. However, the story is more complex than simply gravity acting alone.

Dark matter, a mysterious substance that interacts gravitationally but not electromagnetically, plays a pivotal role. It constitutes about 85% of the matter in the universe and is thought to have formed the underlying scaffolding for galaxies. Simulations suggest that dark matter halos, vast, diffuse distributions of dark matter, formed first. These halos acted as gravitational wells, attracting ordinary matter – the baryonic matter we're familiar with, comprising stars, gas, and dust – into their depths.

This infall of baryonic matter was not uniform. Variations in the density of the dark matter halos led to the formation of clumps and filaments of gas. Within these gas clouds, further gravitational collapse occurred, triggering the birth of the first stars. These initial stars were typically massive and short-lived, producing intense ultraviolet radiation that ionized the surrounding gas, a period known as the Epoch of Reionization. The intense radiation from these first stars likely played a significant role in shaping the subsequent evolution of galaxies.

The early universe was a chaotic environment, with many smaller gas clouds merging and interacting gravitationally. This process of hierarchical structure formation led to the assembly of larger and larger structures, from dwarf galaxies to giant elliptical galaxies. Simulations show that smaller galaxies often merged to form larger ones, a process that continues even today. These mergers have profoundly affected the evolution of galaxies, transforming their morphology, star formation rates, and overall structure. For instance, the merging of gas-rich galaxies can trigger intense bursts of star formation, resulting in a dramatic increase in the galaxy's luminosity.

The specific path a galaxy takes during its evolution depends on a variety of factors, including the initial mass and angular momentum of the gas cloud, the presence of neighboring galaxies, and the rate at which gas flows into the galaxy. The angular momentum plays a significant role in determining the shape of the resulting galaxy. A high angular momentum generally leads to the formation of a rotating disk, resulting in a spiral galaxy, while a low angular momentum results in a more spherical or ellipsoidal structure, characteristic of elliptical galaxies. Gravitational interactions with neighboring galaxies can significantly alter a galaxy's trajectory, triggering mergers, tidal interactions, and disrupting the galaxy's morphology.

The role of dark energy in galaxy evolution, though less directly understood, is equally crucial. Dark energy is a mysterious force that's accelerating the expansion of the universe. This accelerating expansion makes it increasingly difficult for gravity to pull together matter to form new galaxies. The rate of galaxy formation may be decreasing as the universe ages, but it is still ongoing, and some interactions are still occurring.

Observational evidence supports many aspects of the ΛCDM model. Deep surveys of the distant universe, using powerful telescopes like the Hubble Space Telescope and the James Webb Space Telescope, have revealed galaxies at different stages of evolution. These observations allow astronomers to build a clearer picture of galaxy formation and evolution, comparing the observations with simulations. The study of galaxy clusters, vast aggregations of hundreds or thousands of galaxies bound together by gravity, offers valuable insights into the large-scale structure of the universe and the role of dark matter in shaping this structure.

The chemical enrichment of galaxies is another critical aspect of their evolution. As stars live and die, they produce heavier elements through nuclear fusion. When massive stars explode as supernovae, they spew these heavier elements into the interstellar medium, enriching the gas from which new stars will form. This process has gradually increased the metallicity (abundance of heavier elements) of galaxies over time. The chemical composition of a galaxy provides valuable clues about its star formation history and its interactions with its environment.

Observational astronomers employ various techniques to study galaxy formation and evolution. Spectroscopy, for example, allows astronomers to determine the redshift of a galaxy, indicating its distance and thus its age. Spectral analysis also provides information about the chemical composition and kinematics of the galaxy. Infrared and radio observations probe regions obscured by dust, revealing details about the star formation process. Sophisticated image processing techniques allow for the extraction of detailed structural information from galaxy images.

The quest to understand galaxy formation and evolution is an ongoing endeavor. As observational data improves and theoretical models become increasingly sophisticated, our understanding of these complex processes continues to refine. This is a dynamic field, continually evolving as new discoveries are made and our view of the cosmos broadens.

The interplay of gravity, dark matter, dark energy, and the complexities of baryonic matter continue to shape our understanding of the magnificent celestial islands that populate the universe. The study of galaxies is not only about understanding their individual properties, but also about understanding the larger context of their place in the cosmic web, their role in the universe's history, and their ultimate fate. The universe's history is written in the stars, and the galaxies are the chapters in that story. Unraveling this story, page by page, remains a fundamental goal of modern astrophysics. The more we learn, the more the universe reveals its astonishing complexity and beauty, making the quest for knowledge a never-ending, rewarding journey.

Galaxy Clusters and Superclusters

Having established the intricacies of individual galaxy formation and evolution, we now ascend to a grander scale, exploring the cosmic architecture that binds these celestial islands together: galaxy clusters and superclusters. These colossal structures represent the largest gravitationally bound systems in the universe, revealing a level of organization far exceeding the individual lives of galaxies. Instead of viewing galaxies as isolated entities, we must perceive them as components within a vast, interconnected cosmic web.

Galaxy clusters are the first step up in this hierarchical structure. These are dense regions of space containing hundreds to thousands of galaxies, vast quantities of hot, ionized gas, and a significant amount of dark matter. The gravitational pull of this combined mass is immense, holding the galaxies within a relatively compact region, typically spanning tens to hundreds of millions of light-years. The intracluster medium (ICM), the superheated gas residing within a cluster, reaches temperatures of tens of millions of degrees, emitting X-rays detectable by specialized telescopes. This X-ray emission provides crucial information about the cluster's temperature, density, and overall mass distribution. Studying the ICM is vital because it reveals the dynamical processes within the cluster and the distribution of dark matter, which itself doesn't emit or absorb light.

The distribution of galaxies within a cluster isn't random. Many clusters exhibit a central concentration of galaxies, often a giant elliptical galaxy, surrounded by a more diffuse distribution of galaxies towards the cluster's periphery. This central galaxy, sometimes called a brightest cluster galaxy (BCG), is often the most massive galaxy in the cluster, having likely accreted smaller galaxies over time through a process of hierarchical merging. The gravitational interactions within the cluster can trigger tidal forces, leading to distortions in galaxy shapes and the stripping of gas and stars from smaller galaxies as they interact with the denser core. These interactions paint a dynamic picture of a cluster, far from a static collection of galaxies.

Beyond the individual galaxies and the ICM, another crucial player in cluster dynamics is dark matter. Astronomers infer the presence of dark matter in clusters through its gravitational effects on the visible matter, including galaxies and the ICM. Gravitational lensing, a phenomenon where light from distant objects is bent by the gravity of a massive cluster, provides powerful evidence for the existence of dark matter in these structures. The lensing effect subtly distorts the images of background galaxies, allowing astronomers to map the distribution of dark matter within the cluster, revealing a vast halo of unseen mass far exceeding the visible matter. Without the gravitational influence of this substantial dark matter component, the cluster would be unable to maintain its structure and cohesiveness.

Observations of galaxy clusters using different wavelengths of light paint a comprehensive picture of their complex nature. Optical observations reveal the distribution of galaxies themselves, while X-ray observations illuminate the hot gas. Radio observations detect synchrotron radiation from relativistic electrons accelerated by shocks and magnetic fields within the cluster, providing insights into the cluster's dynamical processes and its magnetic field structure. Combining these observations allows astronomers to construct detailed three-dimensional models of galaxy clusters, revealing their complex morphology and the intricate interplay of their components.

The formation of galaxy clusters themselves is a complex process arising from the hierarchical structure formation outlined earlier. Smaller groups of galaxies, known as galaxy groups, merge and coalesce under the influence of gravity, gradually building up larger and larger structures. This hierarchical merging process is not a smooth or uniform event; it's punctuated by chaotic interactions, mergers, and the stripping of material from individual galaxies.

Simulations of galaxy cluster formation, incorporating the effects of dark matter, gravity, and baryonic matter, have been instrumental in understanding these dynamic processes. These simulations have helped researchers predict the abundance of galaxy clusters at different redshifts (and thus at different epochs of the universe's history), confirming that they are indeed the result of this hierarchical merging process.

Moving beyond galaxy clusters, we reach the largest known gravitationally bound structures in the universe: superclusters. These are immense collections of galaxy clusters and groups bound together by gravity, forming massive structures spanning hundreds of millions of light- years. The distribution of superclusters isn't uniform; instead, they tend to be arranged in elongated filaments and sheets, separated by vast voids relatively devoid of galaxies. This large-scale distribution is often referred to as the "cosmic web," a filamentary network spanning the observable universe.

The cosmic web provides a compelling visual representation of the universe's large-scale structure. The filaments and sheets of galaxies are the densest regions, where the majority of galaxies, clusters, and superclusters reside. The voids, in contrast, are vast, nearly empty regions of space between the filaments. The origin and formation of this cosmic web is still a subject of active research, but it's deeply connected to the initial density fluctuations in the early universe. The subtle variations in the density of the early universe, amplified by gravity and dark matter, acted as seeds for the formation of the cosmic web, with denser regions eventually collapsing to form the filaments and sheets of galaxies we observe today.

The Great Wall, a massive supercluster spanning over 500 million light-years, stands as a prominent example of these enormous cosmic structures. Its immense scale dwarfs even the largest galaxy clusters, showcasing the sheer power of gravity on cosmological scales. Other superclusters, like the Perseus-Pisces supercluster and the Shapley Supercluster, further illustrate the dominant role of large-scale gravitational structures in shaping the observable universe. Mapping these superclusters and understanding their dynamics is crucial for refining our cosmological models and understanding the large-scale distribution of matter in the universe.

The study of galaxy clusters and superclusters is not simply an exercise in cataloging cosmic objects. These structures provide valuable insights into fundamental cosmological parameters, such as the density of dark matter and dark energy. By studying the distribution of galaxies and clusters, astronomers can constrain cosmological models and test their predictions. The dynamics of clusters, including the motion of galaxies within the cluster and the properties of the ICM, provide additional clues to the nature of dark matter and its interaction with baryonic matter.

The ongoing exploration of galaxy clusters and superclusters utilizes advanced observational techniques and sophisticated theoretical models. Powerful telescopes, including X-ray telescopes like Chandra and XMM-Newton, and radio telescopes like the Very Large Array (VLA) and the

Atacama Large Millimeter/submillimeter Array (ALMA), are instrumental in observing these distant objects.

Numerical simulations, incorporating the complexities of gravity, dark matter, and hydrodynamics, play a vital role in modeling the formation and evolution of these colossal structures. The combination of these observational and theoretical approaches is steadily refining our understanding of the cosmic web and the organization of matter on the largest scales.

The journey from the individual galaxies to the immense superclusters reveals a universe characterized by a profound hierarchical structure. This structure, born from the subtle density fluctuations of the early universe and shaped by the interplay of gravity, dark matter, and dark energy, continues to captivate and challenge astrophysicists. As we continue to explore and map the cosmic web, we move closer to unveiling the mysteries of the universe's formation and evolution, confirming the remarkable connectedness of all things cosmological. The story of the universe is a story of interconnectedness, a testament to the power of gravity and the remarkable complexity of the cosmos, written not just in the stars but in the vast, intricate tapestry of galaxy clusters and superclusters.

Active Galactic Nuclei and Quasars

Having explored the grand tapestry of galaxy clusters and superclusters, the largest known structures in the universe, we now delve into the intense energy production occurring within individual galaxies themselves. Specifically, we will examine active galactic nuclei (AGN) and their most extreme manifestation: quasars. These objects represent some of the most luminous and enigmatic entities in the cosmos, their energy output dwarfing even the combined light of billions of stars.

The key to understanding AGN lies in recognizing the central role played by supermassive black holes (SMBHs). These behemoths, millions or even billions of times the mass of our Sun, reside at the hearts of many, if not most, galaxies. While SMBHs in quiescent galaxies exert a significant gravitational influence on their surroundings, their role in AGN is far more dynamic and energetic.

In AGN, the SMBH is actively accreting matter – gas, dust, and stars – from its surrounding environment. This infalling material doesn't simply plunge directly into the black hole. Instead, it forms a swirling accretion disk, a structure orbiting the SMBH at incredibly high speeds. The friction within this disk generates immense heat, leading to the emission of radiation across the electromagnetic spectrum, from radio waves to gamma rays.

The energy output of an AGN is truly astounding. It's not just the heat from the accretion disk; the gravitational energy released as matter spirals inward is converted into kinetic energy and eventually into radiation. This process is incredibly efficient, converting a substantial fraction of the infalling matter's mass into energy, in accordance with Einstein's famous equation, $E=mc^2$. This efficiency is far greater than the energy production in stars, which fuse hydrogen into helium, a process that only converts a tiny fraction of the mass into energy.

The accretion process isn't always smooth and steady. The infalling material can become turbulent and clumpy, leading to variations in the AGN's brightness and spectral characteristics. Furthermore, magnetic fields play a crucial role, channeling some of the accreting material into powerful jets that are ejected from the vicinity of the SMBH at near-light speeds. These jets can extend for millions of light- years, impacting the surrounding intergalactic medium and influencing the evolution of the host galaxy.

Observations of AGN reveal a complex and varied population. The observed properties can vary significantly depending on factors such as the accretion rate, the orientation of the accretion disk relative to our line of sight, and the presence and strength of the jets. Some AGN appear as relatively quiet, low-luminosity sources, while others shine with extraordinary brilliance. This diversity has led to a classification scheme based on their observed properties, including their spectral energy distribution and the presence or absence of broad emission lines in their spectra.

Quasars, the most luminous type of AGN, represent the extreme end of this spectrum. They are so bright that their light can outshine the entire host galaxy, making them detectable even at immense cosmological distances. Their immense luminosity is a direct consequence of an extremely high accretion rate onto the central SMBH. This rapid accretion fuels the powerful radiation output, which can easily surpass the total luminosity of the largest galaxies.

The discovery of quasars revolutionized our understanding of the universe. Their immense distances imply that we are observing them as they were billions of years ago, when the universe was much younger. Their high redshift, indicating their significant distance and velocity, reveals that these objects were more common in the early universe than they are today. This suggests that the growth of SMBHs and the prevalence of highly active galactic nuclei were more significant in the early stages of galactic evolution.

Observational techniques for studying AGN and quasars are multifaceted. Optical telescopes provide information on the host galaxy and the broad-line regions surrounding the SMBH. X-ray observations probe the hot gas near the black hole, revealing insights into the accretion process and the surrounding environment. Radio observations are crucial for detecting the jets, mapping their structure and determining their properties. Finally, infrared observations are essential for penetrating dust obscuration, allowing us to study the regions hidden from view at other wavelengths.

The study of AGN and quasars has deep implications for our understanding of galaxy evolution. The energy output from AGN can influence star formation in the host galaxy, triggering or suppressing it depending on the intensity of the feedback mechanisms. The jets launched by AGN can also affect the surrounding intergalactic medium, enriching it with heavy elements and influencing the large-scale structure of the universe. Furthermore, the study of AGN helps to trace the growth of SMBHs over cosmic time, shedding light on the relationship between black hole mass and galaxy properties.

While the fundamental mechanisms of AGN are now reasonably well understood, many questions remain unanswered. For example, the precise mechanisms that regulate the accretion process are still not fully understood. The interplay between the SMBH, the accretion disk, and the jets is incredibly complex, and ongoing research is continually refining our models. Moreover, the role of AGN in galaxy evolution is still being actively investigated.

Unraveling these mysteries requires combining data from various observational techniques and developing sophisticated theoretical models.

The ongoing study of AGN relies heavily on advanced observational facilities. Ground-based telescopes, including extremely large telescopes (ELTs) currently under construction, will provide unprecedented spatial resolution and sensitivity, enabling us to probe the innermost regions of AGN with greater accuracy. Space-based missions, such as future X-ray and gamma-ray observatories, will offer unique perspectives, allowing us to study the high-energy emission from these extreme objects. The synergy between ground- based and space-based observations, combined with advanced theoretical modeling, will undoubtedly lead to significant breakthroughs in our understanding of these fascinating and energetic cosmic phenomena.

The study of AGN and quasars is not merely an academic exercise. These objects are fundamental to our understanding of the universe's evolution and the interconnectedness of galactic processes. From the formation and growth of supermassive black holes to their feedback mechanisms influencing the star formation rate of entire galaxies, understanding AGN unlocks pivotal aspects of cosmic history. This intricate dance between SMBHs and their host galaxies highlights the dynamic nature of the universe, constantly reshaping itself on scales both grand and microscopic. As we continue to explore these extreme objects, we come closer to piecing together the complete story of cosmic evolution, a narrative written in the light of billions of stars and the intense energy of active galactic nuclei and their enigmatic quasars. The ongoing quest to understand AGN represents a continuing chapter in humanity's exploration of the universe, a testament to our enduring curiosity and our drive to unravel the cosmos's most profound mysteries. The journey, however, is far from over, and the next chapter promises to be even more exciting as new observational tools and theoretical insights push the boundaries of our knowledge further into the heart of the cosmic unknown.

The Suns Structure and Composition

Having journeyed to the far reaches of the universe, exploring the energetic hearts of galaxies and the enigmatic quasars they harbor, we now turn our gaze inward, to a celestial body far closer to home: our Sun. While seemingly constant and unchanging in our daily lives, the Sun is a dynamic and complex engine of energy, a star whose life cycle profoundly impacts our own planet's existence.

Understanding its structure and composition is fundamental to grasping the processes that have shaped and continue to shape our solar system.

The Sun, like all stars, is a gigantic ball of plasma, primarily composed of hydrogen and helium. However, the Sun's internal structure is far from uniform. It's layered, much like an onion, each layer possessing unique characteristics and playing a vital role in the star's energy generation and transport. At the very heart lies the core, a region where temperatures reach an astounding 15 million degrees Celsius. This extreme heat and pressure are the catalysts for the nuclear fusion reactions that power the Sun and, indeed, all stars of similar mass.

In the Sun's core, hydrogen atoms are forced together under immense pressure, overcoming the electrostatic repulsion between their positively charged protons. Through a series of nuclear reactions, primarily the proton-proton chain reaction, four hydrogen nuclei fuse to form a single helium nucleus.

This process isn't a perfect conversion; a tiny fraction of the original mass is converted into energy, released as photons— particles of light—and kinetic energy of the resulting particles. This energy production is the source of the Sun's luminosity, the vast outpouring of radiation that bathes our solar system in light and warmth. The sheer scale of these nuclear reactions is mind-boggling; every second, the Sun converts an estimated 4 million tons of matter into energy.

This energy, generated deep within the Sun's core, doesn't immediately escape. Instead, it embarks on a long and arduous journey to the surface. The energy transport is not a simple process; it involves two main mechanisms: radiative diffusion and convection. In the radiative zone, which extends outwards from the core, energy is transported through the absorption and re-emission of photons. The photons are continually absorbed and re-emitted by the plasma particles, gradually making their way outward. This process is remarkably slow; a photon can take hundreds of thousands of years to traverse the radiative zone.

Beyond the radiative zone lies the convective zone, a region where the plasma is less dense and opaque. Here, energy transport shifts from radiative diffusion to convection. Hot plasma rises from the base of the convective zone, carrying energy towards the surface, while cooler plasma sinks to replace it. This churning, bubbling motion is responsible for the granular appearance of the Sun's surface, visible through powerful telescopes. The granulation, characterized by numerous bright cells known as granules, represents the tops of these convective currents. Each granule is about 1,000 kilometers in diameter and has a lifetime of only about 8 minutes, a testament to the dynamic nature of the Sun's outer layers.

The Sun's visible surface is called the photosphere. It's from this layer that most of the Sun's light is emitted, marking the boundary between the opaque interior and the transparent outer layers. The photosphere's temperature is about 5,500 degrees Celsius, considerably cooler than the core but still hot enough to emit intense radiation across the electromagnetic spectrum. The photosphere isn't a perfectly smooth surface; it's marked by sunspots, relatively cool and dark regions associated with intense magnetic activity. These sunspots can be considerably larger than Earth and can appear and disappear over periods of days or weeks.

Above the photosphere lies the chromosphere, a relatively thin layer extending upwards to about 2,000 kilometers.

While much fainter than the photosphere, the chromosphere is visible during total solar eclipses, appearing as a reddish glow around the Sun's limb. Its temperature increases with altitude, reaching thousands of degrees. The chromosphere is also the location of spicules, jet-like eruptions of hot plasma that extend upwards into the corona.

The outermost layer of the Sun is the corona, a vast and tenuous atmosphere that extends millions of kilometers into space. The corona's temperature is remarkably high, reaching millions of degrees Celsius. This incredibly high temperature is a puzzle that continues to fascinate scientists. It's far higher than what's expected based on the Sun's surface temperature, suggesting the existence of mechanisms that efficiently heat the coronal plasma. The corona is the source of the solar wind, a continuous stream of charged particles that flows outward from the Sun, affecting the interplanetary medium and interacting with the atmospheres of planets.

Coronal mass ejections (CMEs), powerful eruptions of plasma and magnetic field lines, are also associated with the corona and can cause significant disturbances in Earth's magnetosphere, leading to geomagnetic storms and auroras.

The Sun's composition is remarkably simple, dominated by hydrogen and helium. By mass, about 71% is hydrogen and 27% is helium. The remaining 2% comprises heavier elements, collectively known as metals in astronomical parlance. This is a crucial aspect of the Sun's properties, as the relative abundance of hydrogen and helium directly influences the rate of nuclear fusion in the core and thus the Sun's energy output.

The elemental abundances within the Sun reflect the conditions in the early universe. Hydrogen and helium were the primary elements formed in the Big Bang, while heavier elements were synthesized later in stars through nuclear fusion. The abundance of heavier elements in the Sun, often expressed as metallicity, provides clues about the Sun's origin and its relationship to the interstellar medium from which it formed. The presence of these heavier elements plays a role in the Sun's internal structure and energy transport, albeit a minor one compared to hydrogen and helium. Careful spectroscopic analysis of sunlight allows astronomers to determine the precise abundances of these elements, providing invaluable insights into the Sun's chemical history. Such analysis has revealed trace amounts of elements such as oxygen, carbon, nitrogen, and iron.

Although present in much smaller quantities than hydrogen and helium, these elements nevertheless contribute to the complexity of the Sun's chemical composition and play various roles in its overall dynamics. Their presence also underscores the intricate connection between the Sun and the broader galactic environment, a testament to the cosmic recycling of matter that has shaped the universe as we know it.

The study of the Sun's structure and composition is not merely an academic pursuit; it's vital for understanding the Sun's influence on Earth and the broader solar system. Solar flares, coronal mass ejections, and variations in the solar wind can have significant effects on Earth's climate, communication systems, and power grids. A deeper understanding of the Sun's internal processes is therefore crucial for developing effective space weather forecasting and mitigating the potential impacts of solar activity. Furthermore, understanding the Sun's evolution sheds light on the evolution of other stars and the formation of planetary systems. By studying our own Sun, we gain a fundamental understanding of stellar processes that occur throughout the universe. The Sun, although just one star amongst billions, serves as a critical window into the remarkable physics and chemistry that shape our cosmos, a celestial laboratory ever- present in our sky, its energy sustaining life as we know it.

The quest to unravel its mysteries, and those of all stars, continues to be a compelling force driving astronomical research, promising further fascinating discoveries in the decades to come.

Solar Activity Sunspots Flares and Coronal Mass Ejections

Our understanding of the Sun's internal dynamics provides a crucial foundation for comprehending its dynamic surface and the various forms of solar activity that emanate from it. While the Sun may appear relatively calm to the casual observer, its surface and outer atmosphere are far from static. Instead, they are a theater of dramatic events, driven by the complex interplay of plasma flows, magnetic fields, and the immense energy generated within the star's core. These events, collectively known as solar activity, range from relatively minor disturbances to powerful eruptions that can have significant consequences for Earth and the entire solar system.

One of the most readily observable manifestations of solar activity is the appearance of sunspots. These are dark, relatively cool regions on the Sun's photosphere, appearing dark only by contrast to the surrounding, brighter areas.

Their "coolness" is relative; while their temperatures still reach several thousand degrees Celsius, they are significantly cooler than the surrounding photosphere, resulting in their darker appearance. Sunspots aren't simply dark patches; they are complex structures characterized by intense magnetic fields, often many times stronger than the Sun's average magnetic field. These intense magnetic fields inhibit the convective flow of plasma, reducing the energy transport to the surface and leading to the lower temperatures observed in sunspots.

The appearance of sunspots is intricately linked to the Sun's magnetic field. The Sun's magnetic field is far from uniform; it's constantly evolving and changing, driven by the turbulent motions within the convective zone. As the Sun rotates, differential rotation—a phenomenon where the Sun's equator rotates faster than its poles—stretches and twists the magnetic field lines. This twisting and tangling of magnetic field lines can lead to the formation of magnetic flux tubes, which eventually break through the surface, creating sunspots. Often, sunspots appear in pairs or groups, with the magnetic polarity of each spot opposite to its partner, reflecting the underlying magnetic structure.

The number of sunspots visible on the Sun's surface varies over time, following an approximately 11-year cycle known as the solar cycle. This cycle is characterized by a period of increasing sunspot activity, reaching a maximum known as solar maximum, followed by a period of decreasing activity, culminating in a solar minimum. During solar maximum, the Sun's surface can be covered with numerous sunspots, while during solar minimum, few or even no sunspots may be visible. The precise mechanisms driving the solar cycle are still under investigation, but it is believed to be related to the complex dynamics of the Sun's magnetic field and the internal processes that generate and sustain it. The solar cycle has significant implications for space weather, with increased solar activity during solar maximum leading to a greater frequency of solar flares and coronal mass ejections.

Beyond sunspots, the Sun exhibits other forms of activity, most notably solar flares. Solar flares are sudden, intense bursts of energy released from the Sun's atmosphere, often associated with sunspots and their complex magnetic fields. These flares release immense amounts of radiation across the electromagnetic spectrum, from radio waves to gamma rays. The energy released during a large solar flare can be equivalent to billions of megatons of TNT, highlighting the immense power of these events. The radiation emitted during a solar flare can reach Earth within minutes, potentially disrupting radio communications and satellite operations. The exact mechanism triggering solar flares is not fully understood, but it is thought to involve the sudden release of magnetic energy stored in the Sun's atmosphere, possibly caused by the reconnection of magnetic field lines.

Coronal mass ejections (CMEs) are another significant form of solar activity. Unlike solar flares, which primarily release radiation, CMEs involve the ejection of vast quantities of plasma and magnetic field from the Sun's corona. These eruptions can propel billions of tons of plasma into space at speeds of millions of kilometers per hour. CMEs can be associated with solar flares, but they can also occur independently. The interaction between a CME and Earth's magnetosphere can have significant consequences, triggering geomagnetic storms. These storms can disrupt power grids, damage satellites, and interfere with radio communications. Furthermore, the interaction between CMEs and Earth's atmosphere can result in stunning auroral displays, also known as the Northern and Southern Lights, as charged particles from the CME interact with the Earth's atmosphere.

The impact of solar activity on Earth is a critical area of study, as it can have far-reaching effects on technological infrastructure and human activities. Space weather forecasting, which aims to predict solar events and their potential impact on Earth, is becoming increasingly important. Scientists use a variety of techniques, including monitoring sunspots, solar flares, and CMEs through various instruments, such as satellites and ground-based telescopes. By analyzing these observations, scientists can develop models that help predict the likelihood and intensity of future solar events. Understanding the underlying physics governing solar activity is also crucial for developing effective mitigation strategies to protect critical infrastructure from the potential impacts of space weather.

The study of solar activity is not only crucial for protecting our technological systems but also for understanding the Sun's overall dynamics and its role in shaping the interplanetary environment. The Sun's activity influences the interplanetary magnetic field, the solar wind, and the distribution of energetic particles throughout the solar system. These aspects play a crucial role in shaping the environments of planets, influencing their atmospheres and potentially even affecting the evolution of life. The long- term variations in solar activity, such as changes in the solar cycle, also have implications for understanding climate change on Earth, though the extent of this influence is still a subject of ongoing research and debate.

The Sun's dynamic nature, reflected in its various forms of activity, underscores its complex and ever-evolving nature. Sunspots, solar flares, and coronal mass ejections are merely some of the manifestations of the Sun's powerful energy output and its intricate magnetic field. These events, while sometimes disruptive, are also essential aspects of the Sun's life cycle and its influence on the solar system. Continued research and observation are vital to further understanding these phenomena, improving space weather forecasting capabilities, and mitigating the potential impacts of solar activity on our increasingly technology-dependent society.

The Sun, our nearest star, remains a captivating and constantly surprising object of study, revealing new facets of its behavior with each passing year, reminding us of the powerful and dynamic forces at play in our cosmic neighborhood. The detailed study of these solar phenomena not only expands our fundamental understanding of stellar processes but also provides crucial insights into how these processes impact our planet and our technological systems. The ongoing quest to unravel the intricate mechanisms driving solar activity is a compelling and ever-evolving field of astrophysical research, with far-reaching implications for both scientific advancement and societal preparedness. The Sun, a seemingly constant beacon in our sky, is, in reality, a highly active and variable star whose influence on Earth and the wider solar system continues to shape our understanding of the cosmos.

The Suns Energy Production Nuclear Fusion

Having explored the Sun's dynamic surface and the various manifestations of its activity, we now delve into the heart of the matter: the Sun's energy production. This incredible powerhouse, a seemingly constant and unwavering presence in our sky, is fueled by a process of unimaginable scale and power: nuclear fusion. Unlike the fission reactions used in nuclear power plants on Earth, which split atomic nuclei, nuclear fusion combines atomic nuclei, releasing vast amounts of energy in the process. This is the process that sustains the Sun and gives it its luminosity, warmth, and life- giving energy.

The Sun's core, a region extending to about 25% of its radius, is where this fusion takes place. The conditions here are extreme: temperatures reach approximately 15 million degrees Celsius, and the density is about 150 times that of water. These extraordinary conditions are essential for initiating and sustaining the nuclear fusion reactions. The primary fuel for this reaction is hydrogen, specifically the most abundant isotope, protium, which consists of a single proton. Through a series of complex steps, these protons are fused together to form helium, releasing tremendous amounts of energy in the form of photons (light particles) and neutrinos (nearly massless subatomic particles).

The dominant process powering the Sun's energy output is the proton-proton chain reaction (pp chain). This chain reaction, while seemingly simple in its overall description, involves several intricate steps, each governed by the laws of nuclear physics and probability. The pp chain begins with the collision of two protons. The probability of two protons fusing directly into a stable helium nucleus is incredibly low, due to the electrostatic repulsion between their positive charges. However, under the extreme conditions of the Sun's core, the protons possess sufficient kinetic energy to overcome this repulsion, albeit infrequently.

When two protons collide with sufficient energy, one of them undergoes beta-plus decay, transforming into a neutron while emitting a positron (the antiparticle of an electron) and a neutrino. This transforms the two protons into a deuteron, which is the nucleus of deuterium (heavy hydrogen), consisting of one proton and one neutron. The positron quickly annihilates with an electron, releasing two gamma- ray photons. The neutrino, on the other hand, is weakly interacting, meaning it can pass almost unimpeded through the Sun's immense mass, carrying away a small fraction of the energy produced. This energy loss, although seemingly minor, is essential for understanding the Sun's overall energy balance and luminosity.

The deuteron, now formed, is far more likely to interact with another proton than two protons were initially. In a relatively short period, a deuteron and a proton will fuse, forming a helium-3 nucleus (two protons and one neutron) and releasing a gamma-ray photon. This gamma-ray photon, like the previous ones, is highly energetic and contributes to the immense energy flux within the Sun's core.

There are different branches that the pp chain can take from this point, depending on the further interactions. The most common outcome involves two helium-3 nuclei fusing to form a helium-4 nucleus (two protons and two neutrons), releasing two protons in the process. This is the final stage of the most prevalent pp chain, producing one helium-4 nucleus (also known as an alpha particle) from four protons. The net result of this process is the conversion of four protons into one helium-4 nucleus, with the release of two positrons, two neutrinos, and several gamma-ray photons.

The energy released in the pp chain comes primarily from the mass difference between four protons and one helium-4 nucleus. According to Einstein's famous equation, $E=mc^2$, mass and energy are equivalent. A small amount of mass is converted into a tremendous amount of energy during the fusion process, powering the Sun's immense luminosity. This mass deficit, however small it may seem, is the source of the Sun's incredible energy output, sustaining its radiation for billions of years.

The energy generated within the Sun's core doesn't immediately reach the surface. It undergoes a long and complex journey, traveling through the radiative zone and the convective zone. In the radiative zone, energy is transported primarily through the absorption and re-emission of photons, a relatively slow process. Photons continuously interact with the plasma, scattering and changing direction, making their journey to the surface extraordinarily long. It's estimated that a photon takes hundreds of thousands, even millions of years, to reach the Sun's surface from its core.

Once the energy reaches the convective zone, the process becomes more efficient. Here, hot plasma rises to the surface, carrying energy with it, and cooler plasma sinks. This convective motion dramatically accelerates the transport of energy, allowing it to reach the surface relatively quickly compared to the radiative zone's sluggish process.

The energy finally emerges from the Sun's surface in the form of light and heat, illuminating and warming our planet.

The energy output of the Sun, as a result of the pp chain, is remarkably stable. However, small variations do occur, influencing the Sun's activity and impacting the Earth. These variations, while relatively small compared to the overall energy output, are crucial in understanding solar cycles and space weather phenomena. The precise mechanisms regulating this stability are still an active area of research, and sophisticated computer simulations are continuously developed to unravel the complexities of stellar nucleosynthesis.

The study of the Sun's energy production is not just of academic interest. Understanding the pp chain and the nuclear reactions within the Sun's core is crucial for comprehending stellar evolution, the formation of elements in the universe, and the ultimate fate of stars. Furthermore, this knowledge informs research into fusion power on Earth, which could potentially provide a clean and sustainable source of energy for future generations. Harnessing the power of nuclear fusion, the same process that powers the Sun, represents one of the most ambitious and potentially transformative endeavors in human history. While still in its early stages, the quest to replicate this process on Earth holds immense promise for addressing the global energy challenge. This pursuit demands an ever-deepening understanding of the fundamental physics governing nuclear fusion, a journey that is intrinsically linked to our continuing exploration of the Sun and its remarkable energy production.

Beyond the pp chain, other fusion reactions can occur in the Sun's core, albeit at much lower rates. These reactions, while less significant in terms of overall energy production, provide valuable insights into the Sun's composition and evolution. These secondary reactions also contribute to the production of heavier elements, adding to the complexity of the Sun's internal processes and the fascinating interplay of nuclear reactions within its core. The details of these less prevalent reactions highlight the sophisticated nature of stellar nucleosynthesis, constantly refining our understanding of the Sun's energy generation mechanism.

The study of the Sun's energy production represents a fascinating intersection of several scientific disciplines, from nuclear physics to astrophysics and plasma physics. It is a testament to the power of scientific inquiry and the remarkable ability of scientists to unravel the secrets of the universe, one proton and one reaction at a time. The ongoing investigation into the Sun's core, with its extreme conditions and complex interactions, is pushing the boundaries of human knowledge and constantly challenging our assumptions about the cosmos. The quest to understand this stellar furnace will continue for decades to come, constantly driving us toward a richer and more profound understanding of the universe and our place within it. The Sun, in its incredible power and complexity, remains a powerful source of inspiration and a profound enigma simultaneously.

The Suns Evolution and Future

Our understanding of the Sun's energy production, as detailed in the previous section, is crucial to comprehending its past, present, and future. The nuclear fusion furnace at its core, primarily driven by the proton-proton chain reaction, isn't merely a static process; it's a dynamic engine whose output slowly changes over vast stretches of time, sculpting the Sun's evolution and ultimately dictating its destiny.

The Sun, like all stars, isn't born fully formed. It began its life as a vast, swirling cloud of gas and dust, primarily hydrogen and helium, left over from the Big Bang and enriched by the remnants of previous generations of stars. This nebula, under the influence of gravity, began to collapse, its density increasing and its temperature soaring. As the cloud contracted, it spun faster, eventually forming a rotating disk with a denser core. This core continued to collapse and heat until the temperature and pressure reached a critical point – around 15 million degrees Celsius – igniting the nuclear fusion reactions at the heart of its existence. This marked the Sun's birth as a main-sequence star, a phase that it has remained in for approximately 4.6 billion years.

The main sequence phase is the longest and most stable period in a star's life. During this time, the Sun maintains a relatively constant luminosity and size, primarily because the inward pull of gravity is balanced by the outward pressure generated by the fusion reactions in its core. This equilibrium, however delicate, ensures a remarkably stable energy output, vital for the existence of life on Earth. The Sun has been diligently converting hydrogen into helium throughout this period, slowly but steadily consuming its primary fuel source.

However, this process of hydrogen fusion is not indefinitely sustainable. As the Sun burns through its hydrogen fuel, the core gradually becomes richer in helium. Helium, being less easily fused than hydrogen, doesn't participate significantly in the energy-generating processes. Consequently, the core contracts, increasing the temperature and pressure. This, in turn, causes the outer layers of the Sun to expand. The Sun isn't merely getting hotter; it's also growing larger.

This marks the beginning of the Sun's transition into a red giant, a dramatic and transformative phase in its life cycle. As the core contracts and heats up, the outer layers expand enormously, engulfing the inner planets, possibly even extending as far as the orbit of Mars. During this phase, the Sun's surface temperature decreases, giving it a reddish hue. The increase in size dramatically increases the Sun's surface area, and while the core's fusion rate increases, the overall luminosity is distributed over a much larger surface, leading to a lower surface temperature.

This transition is not instantaneous. It is a gradual process that will unfold over millions of years. The Sun's luminosity will gradually increase, leading to significant changes in the Earth's climate. This is not a pleasant prospect for life as we know it; the increased solar radiation would make the Earth's surface far too hot to support life. Oceans will evaporate, and the atmosphere will be radically altered.

The expansion into a red giant will also result in changes to the Sun's structure. The convective zone, currently only present in the outer layers, will extend much deeper, leading to a more efficient mixing of materials within the star. This will affect the distribution of elements throughout the Sun, potentially influencing the characteristics of its eventual demise.

After its red giant phase, the Sun will face a final, dramatic phase. When most of the hydrogen in the core is depleted and helium fusion starts, the core will undergo further contraction. The outer layers of the Sun will be expelled, forming a planetary nebula – a luminous shell of gas and dust surrounding a dying star. This beautiful, ethereal structure, often resembling a butterfly or a cosmic flower, is a testament to the Sun's once mighty power. The expelled material will eventually enrich the interstellar medium, contributing to the formation of new stars and planets.

The remaining core of the Sun, now devoid of its outer layers, will collapse into a white dwarf – a small, dense, incredibly hot remnant. This white dwarf will be roughly the size of Earth, but with a mass comparable to the Sun. Its extreme density is a result of electron degeneracy pressure, a quantum mechanical effect that prevents further collapse.

The white dwarf will slowly cool and fade over trillions of years, eventually becoming a cold, dark ember in the vastness of space.

The Sun's journey from a stellar nursery to a white dwarf is a testament to the power of nuclear physics and the cyclical nature of the universe. Its life cycle is not unique; countless stars across the cosmos follow similar paths, each contributing to the cosmic dance of creation and destruction. Understanding this cycle, and the Sun's place within it, allows us to appreciate the finite, yet magnificent, lifespan of our star and the profound implications it has for the fate of our planet and its inhabitants.

The timescale involved in the Sun's evolution is truly immense, stretching across billions of years. While the expansion into a red giant is still billions of years in the future, it serves as a stark reminder of the temporary nature of our cosmic home. The Sun's eventual demise is an unavoidable event, though thankfully one far removed from our current reality.

The study of stellar evolution, including the Sun's predicted path, relies heavily on sophisticated computer models that simulate the complex interplay of gravity, pressure, temperature, and nuclear reactions within a star. These models are constantly refined as our understanding of stellar physics deepens, providing increasingly accurate predictions of the Sun's future. Astronomical observations of other stars in various stages of their life cycle also play a crucial role in verifying and validating these models. By studying these "stellar fossils," we can glimpse into our Sun's potential future, gaining a deeper appreciation for the processes governing stellar evolution and the ultimate fate of stars.

Moreover, the study of the Sun's life cycle is deeply connected to the larger question of the formation and evolution of planetary systems. The Sun's influence extends far beyond its immediate vicinity, shaping the conditions in the solar system and influencing the evolution of the planets. The Sun's past activity, evidenced by solar flares and coronal mass ejections, has profoundly impacted the atmospheres and surface conditions of the planets. Similarly, the Sun's future evolution, particularly its expansion into a red giant, will have catastrophic consequences for the inner planets, fundamentally altering their environments.

The Sun's future evolution will not only have implications for the planets of our solar system; it also has profound implications for our understanding of the universe as a whole. The fate of stars, their deaths and their ultimate contributions to the interstellar medium, are integral parts of the cosmic cycle. The heavy elements forged in the hearts of dying stars, including our own Sun, become the building blocks for future generations of stars and planets. In this sense, the Sun's death is not an end but a continuation of a continuous cycle of stellar birth, life, and death. The Sun's legacy, far from being a somber finale, is a crucial contribution to the ongoing story of the cosmos. The elements that make up our bodies, our planet, and indeed everything around us were originally forged in the heart of stars, a humbling testament to our cosmic origins.

The Suns Influence on the Solar System

The Sun's immense gravitational pull is the architect of our solar system, dictating the orbits of planets, asteroids, comets, and even the dust grains scattered throughout interplanetary space. This force, governed by Newton's law of universal gravitation, holds the solar system together, preventing its constituent parts from flying off into the vast expanse of interstellar space. The strength of the Sun's gravity diminishes with distance, following an inverse- square law, meaning the gravitational pull weakens significantly as you move farther from the Sun. This explains why the inner, rocky planets orbit much faster than the outer, gas giants. Mercury, the closest planet, whips around the Sun in a mere 88 Earth days, a testament to the Sun's powerful gravitational grip at close range. In contrast, Neptune, the most distant planet, takes a leisurely 165 Earth years to complete a single orbit, a testament to the weaker pull of the Sun at its far-flung location.

This gravitational dominance isn't just about orbital periods; it also dictates the shape of planetary orbits. While idealized orbits are perfect ellipses, the real orbits of planets are subtly perturbed by the gravitational influence of other celestial bodies. The giant planets, particularly Jupiter and Saturn, exert noticeable gravitational tugs on the inner planets, leading to slight variations in their orbital paths. These gravitational interactions, while subtle, are crucial for understanding long-term orbital evolution and can even lead to dramatic orbital changes over vast timescales. For example, the gravitational interplay between planets has likely influenced the formation and evolution of asteroid belts, and the dynamics of cometary orbits.

Beyond the planets, the Sun's gravitational reach extends to the countless asteroids and comets that inhabit our solar system. The asteroid belt, located between Mars and Jupiter, is a testament to the Sun's gravitational influence. These rocky remnants of planet formation are trapped in a relatively stable orbit around the Sun, though their paths are constantly influenced by the gravitational pulls of the planets, particularly Jupiter. Comets, on the other hand, hail from far more distant regions of our solar system – the Kuiper Belt and the Oort Cloud – but their paths are eventually steered by the Sun's gravitational field, bringing them inwards towards the inner solar system where we can observe their spectacular displays of dust and gas. The gravitational interactions between the Sun, planets, and comets contribute to the dynamic and ever-changing nature of our solar system.

However, the Sun's influence extends far beyond its gravitational field. The Sun is a dynamic, constantly active star that emits a constant stream of charged particles known as the solar wind. This wind, a supersonic flow of plasma, carries with it the Sun's magnetic field, creating a vast bubble of magnetic influence called the heliosphere, which encompasses the entire solar system. This heliosphere acts as a shield against the interstellar medium, the tenuous gas and dust that permeate the space between stars. The solar wind's interaction with the planets' atmospheres and magnetic fields produces stunning and significant effects.

Planetary atmospheres play a crucial role in mediating the Sun's impact. For planets with significant magnetic fields, like Earth, Jupiter, and Saturn, the interaction is complex but relatively benign. The magnetosphere, a protective bubble generated by the planet's magnetic field, deflects much of the solar wind, preventing it from directly impacting the atmosphere. The interaction between the solar wind and the magnetosphere results in spectacular auroral displays at the poles, as charged particles from the solar wind are channeled along magnetic field lines towards the atmosphere. These auroras are beautiful displays of light, often visible in high- latitude regions, but they also signify a powerful interaction between the Sun and a planet's magnetic shield.

Planets without substantial magnetic fields, like Mars and Venus, lack this level of protection. The solar wind directly interacts with their upper atmospheres, leading to a process known as atmospheric erosion. Over billions of years, the solar wind has stripped away much of the Martian atmosphere, leaving behind a thin and tenuous shell. This process highlights the crucial role that magnetic fields play in protecting planetary atmospheres from the relentless erosion caused by the solar wind. The study of these interactions provides valuable insights into the evolution of planetary atmospheres and the conditions necessary for the development and sustenance of life.

Furthermore, the Sun's influence on the solar system is not uniform or constant. Solar activity is characterized by cycles of increasing and decreasing intensity, with peaks and troughs that occur approximately every 11 years. These solar cycles are driven by changes in the Sun's magnetic field, which influence the frequency and intensity of solar flares and coronal mass ejections (CMEs). Solar flares are sudden bursts of energy that can release vast amounts of radiation, while CMEs are massive expulsions of plasma and magnetic field from the Sun's corona. Both solar flares and CMEs can significantly impact the Earth and other planets, causing disturbances in their magnetospheres, disrupting radio communications, and potentially damaging satellites.

The intensity of these solar events fluctuates throughout the solar cycle. During periods of high solar activity, the frequency and intensity of flares and CMEs are dramatically increased, leading to heightened levels of space weather.

This space weather can have significant consequences for technological infrastructure on Earth, potentially damaging satellites, power grids, and communication systems. The study of solar activity and its implications for space weather is of paramount importance for ensuring the safety and reliability of our technological systems and understanding potential risks to human activities in space.

The Sun's past activity has also left its mark on the surfaces and atmospheres of planets. Evidence suggests that the early Sun, during its infancy, emitted significantly higher levels of radiation and solar wind than it does today. This could have played a role in shaping the evolution of planetary atmospheres and the development of early life on Earth.

Understanding the Sun's past activity helps us to reconstruct the history of the solar system and the conditions under which life arose on our planet. Similarly, predicting future solar activity will help us to mitigate the potential effects of space weather on our technologically advanced society.

In conclusion, the Sun's influence on the solar system is profound and multifaceted, extending far beyond its simple gravitational dominance. The Sun's energy production, its solar wind, and its dynamic activity all play critical roles in shaping the orbits, atmospheres, and magnetospheres of the planets and other objects within the solar system. The Sun is not just a distant star; it is an active, dynamic entity whose interactions with its planetary family are essential to their ongoing evolution. Its power, both gravitational and energetic, is the defining force of our solar system, and its study remains a crucial aspect of our understanding of the cosmos and our place within it. The ongoing research into the Sun's influence continues to unravel the complexities of our solar system and provides vital knowledge for protecting our technological infrastructure and understanding the long- term evolution of our cosmic neighbourhood.

Methods of Detecting Exoplanets

The search for exoplanets, planets orbiting stars other than our Sun, has revolutionized our understanding of planetary systems. Until relatively recently, our knowledge of planets was limited to the eight within our own solar system. The discovery of thousands of exoplanets has shattered this limited perspective, revealing a breathtaking diversity of planetary systems far beyond our wildest imaginings. This astonishing discovery has been made possible by the development of increasingly sophisticated techniques for detecting these distant worlds, each with its own strengths and limitations.

One of the most successful methods for detecting exoplanets is the **transit method** . This technique relies on the subtle dimming of a star's light as a planet passes in front of it, from our perspective here on Earth. Imagine a tiny speck— the planet—passing across the face of a much larger light source—the star. This transit causes a minuscule, but measurable, dip in the star's brightness. By carefully monitoring the brightness of thousands of stars over extended periods, astronomers can identify these periodic dips and infer the presence of an orbiting planet.

The transit method's effectiveness is directly linked to the geometry of the system. The planet's orbit must be aligned in such a way that it transits across the face of its star from our viewpoint. This geometric constraint limits the number of transiting planets we can detect. However, the Kepler space telescope, specifically designed to employ this method, has discovered thousands of exoplanets. The success of Kepler highlights the efficacy of the transit method when applied on a large scale. The size of the dip in brightness is directly related to the size of the planet, allowing astronomers to estimate the planet's radius. The time between transits provides information about the planet's orbital period, giving an indication of its distance from its host star.

However, the transit method has inherent limitations. For instance, it is biased towards detecting large planets that orbit close to their stars, as these produce more easily detectable brightness dips. Furthermore, the method relies on precise measurements of stellar brightness, requiring high- quality data and careful analysis to eliminate other potential sources of dimming, such as stellar activity or the presence of binary companion stars. It's also challenging to determine a planet's mass using the transit method alone, requiring further observations using complementary techniques.

Another highly successful method is the **radial velocity method** , also known as the Doppler spectroscopy method. This method exploits the subtle wobble of a star caused by the gravitational pull of an orbiting planet. As a planet orbits its star, its gravitational influence causes the star to move slightly back and forth. This stellar wobble can be detected by observing the Doppler shift in the star's light. When the star moves towards us, its light is blueshifted (shifted towards shorter wavelengths), and when it moves away, its light is redshifted (shifted towards longer wavelengths). By meticulously analyzing these shifts, astronomers can infer the presence of an orbiting planet and even estimate its mass.

The radial velocity method is particularly sensitive to massive planets orbiting close to their stars, making it complementary to the transit method. It is less sensitive to geometric constraints than the transit method, as it can detect planets regardless of orbital orientation. However, it is more challenging to detect smaller planets or planets in wider orbits using this method, as the stellar wobble they induce is smaller and therefore harder to measure with current technology. This method also requires highly precise spectroscopic measurements, demanding advanced instrumentation and sophisticated data analysis techniques.

Direct imaging, though a conceptually simple method, represents a considerable technological challenge. It involves directly observing the planet's light, separated from the overwhelming light of its host star. This is exceptionally difficult because stars are vastly brighter than their planets.

To achieve this, astronomers must employ sophisticated techniques such as coronagraphs, which block the starlight, and adaptive optics, which compensate for the blurring effects of Earth's atmosphere.

While direct imaging provides the most direct evidence of an exoplanet's existence, it is currently limited to detecting large planets orbiting far from their stars. The planets must be sufficiently far from their stars to allow their faint light to be distinguished from the intense glare of their parent stars.

This method is also significantly influenced by the presence of dust disks around stars, which can obscure the planet's light. Direct imaging is therefore currently biased towards detecting large, young, and hot gas giant planets at a significant distance from their host stars. Technological advancements in both telescope size and instrumentation are continually expanding the capabilities of this method.

Finally, **gravitational microlensing** provides a unique approach to detecting exoplanets. This method relies on the effect of gravitational lensing, where the gravity of a massive object, such as a star or planet, bends and magnifies the light from a more distant star. When a star with a planetary system passes in front of a more distant star, the gravity of the star and its planets can cause a temporary brightening of the background star's light. The specific pattern of this brightening can reveal the presence of planets.

Gravitational microlensing has the advantage of being sensitive to planets of a wide range of masses and orbital distances. It is also less sensitive to geometric constraints than the transit method. However, it is a statistical method, meaning that the events are unpredictable and relatively rare. Therefore, it's challenging to conduct follow-up observations to confirm the presence of planets and determine their properties. Microlensing events are only fleeting, lasting from a few days to several weeks, so timing is critical. The detection of a planet via this method depends on a fortunate alignment of stars and the presence of a sufficiently massive object along the line of sight to create a detectable lensing effect.

In conclusion, the hunt for exoplanets involves a diverse array of detection methods, each with its own strengths, weaknesses, and biases. The transit method is efficient for discovering relatively large, close-in planets; the radial velocity method is effective for finding massive planets regardless of orbital inclination. Direct imaging offers the clearest images but is limited to large, distant planets.

Gravitational microlensing has unique sensitivity to a broader range of planets but is limited by the rarity of events. The synergy between these methods, using complementary techniques to confirm findings and expand the scope of discovery, is essential for continually refining our understanding of exoplanetary systems and the prevalence of planets throughout the universe. The development of new technologies, such as extremely large telescopes and sophisticated space-based observatories, continues to improve the sensitivity and reach of each of these techniques, promising further exciting discoveries in the years to come. This ongoing exploration promises to reveal more about the diversity and prevalence of planetary systems, expanding our knowledge of the cosmos and potentially leading to the discovery of other habitable worlds.

Types of Exoplanets Hot Jupiters SuperEarths and More

The discovery of thousands of exoplanets has not only confirmed the existence of planets beyond our solar system but has also revealed a stunning diversity in their properties. Unlike our relatively orderly solar system, with its well- defined categories of terrestrial and gas giant planets, exoplanets present a much richer tapestry of worlds. This section delves into some of the most intriguing types of exoplanets, showcasing the astonishing variety found across the cosmos.

One of the most surprising discoveries has been the prevalence of **hot Jupiters** . These are gas giant planets, similar in mass to Jupiter but orbiting incredibly close to their host stars. Their orbital periods can be just a few days, meaning a "year" on a hot Jupiter is only a few Earth days long. The proximity to their stars results in extremely high surface temperatures, often exceeding 1,000 degrees Celsius. These scorching temperatures preclude the existence of liquid water and any life as we know it. However, their existence challenges our initial models of planetary formation, as it's difficult to explain how such massive planets could form so close to their stars. Current theories suggest migration – a process where planets gradually move closer to their star over time due to gravitational interactions with the protoplanetary disk or other planets in the system.

The high temperatures of hot Jupiters also lead to interesting atmospheric phenomena. Observations have revealed inflated atmospheres, meaning the radius of these planets is significantly larger than expected for their mass. This inflation is likely caused by the intense stellar irradiation heating the upper atmosphere, causing it to expand. Furthermore, the intense heat can lead to the formation of exotic molecules and atmospheric dynamics far different from those found in our own solar system's gas giants.

Detailed spectroscopic studies are helping astronomers unveil the complex compositions of hot Jupiter atmospheres, providing insights into the formation and evolution of these unique worlds. For example, observations have detected a wide range of elements in hot Jupiter atmospheres, including metals like sodium, potassium, and even titanium, suggesting that the atmospheric processes are far from simple. The detection of water vapor, though common, has also raised questions about the abundance and distribution of water in these systems and its implications for our understanding of planetary formation mechanisms.

In contrast to the gas giants found close to their stars, many exoplanets are discovered significantly farther out. Some are even located in regions analogous to our own Kuiper Belt.

These planets, often referred to as **cold Jupiters** , while having similar masses and compositions to Jupiter, exhibit radically different atmospheric conditions due to their frigid temperatures. However, their detection and characterization are significantly more challenging due to their faintness and larger orbital periods. Technological advancements in telescope capabilities and observational techniques will be necessary to conduct in-depth analyses of their atmospheres and gain a better understanding of their properties. The search for cold Jupiters promises to yield vital information about the formation processes and dynamics within planetary systems, and their very existence sheds light on the diversity of orbital configurations in the cosmos.

Another fascinating class of exoplanets is **super-Earths** . These planets are larger than Earth but smaller than Neptune. Their composition varies significantly, ranging from rocky worlds with substantial atmospheres to planets with significant amounts of water or even ice. The term "super- Earth" refers purely to their size and doesn't imply any similarity to Earth in terms of habitability. In fact, many super-Earths orbit their stars within the habitable zone, the region where liquid water could exist on the surface, but their atmospheric conditions and composition remain uncertain. Some super-Earths might possess thick, dense atmospheres, leading to intense surface pressures and high temperatures, rendering them uninhabitable. Others may have thin atmospheres or even none at all, exposing their surfaces to the harsh radiation from their star. The diversity of super-Earths necessitates further investigation to ascertain their atmospheric compositions, surface temperatures, and overall habitability.

The detection and characterization of super-Earths present unique challenges. Their relatively small size compared to gas giants makes them harder to detect using some methods, like the transit method. However, advanced techniques and telescopes continually enhance our ability to detect and study these potentially habitable worlds. The determination of a super-Earth's composition and atmospheric properties depends on sophisticated modeling techniques and detailed observations, particularly spectroscopic data analysis. Future missions and the development of larger telescopes will play a crucial role in further characterizing super-Earths and refining our understanding of their habitability. The discovery of super-Earths has significantly expanded our understanding of the diversity of planetary systems and the prevalence of potentially habitable worlds beyond our solar system.

Beyond hot Jupiters and super-Earths, the exoplanet catalog includes other unusual and intriguing planetary types. **Mini-Neptunes**, for example, are smaller than Neptune but larger than Earth, with thick atmospheres composed primarily of hydrogen and helium. These planets bridge the gap between the icy giants in our solar system and the smaller, rocky planets. The properties of mini-Neptunes differ significantly from both, raising questions about their formation processes and the role of atmospheric conditions in their evolution.

Understanding the formation and evolution of these planets requires considering different parameters, including their initial mass, accretion rates, and the influence of their host star. These questions highlight the need for advanced modeling and observational techniques to fully grasp the processes governing the diversity of exoplanetary compositions.

Then there are the **water worlds** , hypothetical planets dominated by water. These planets are believed to have substantial amounts of water, possibly more than Earth, either in liquid, solid (ice), or gaseous forms. Their exact composition and habitability remain uncertain, depending on the atmospheric composition, internal structure and temperature. The presence of water, however, makes them a prime candidate for future research concerning the potential for extraterrestrial life. The existence of water worlds would further broaden our understanding of the diverse environments that can exist in other planetary systems, highlighting the significant role of water in the formation and evolution of planetary bodies.

Finally, the discovery of exoplanets orbiting binary star systems, known as **circumbinary planets** , challenges our understanding of planetary formation in more complex environments. These planets orbit both stars in the system, navigating a complex gravitational field. Their stability is contingent on a balance between the gravitational forces from both stars. The very existence of circumbinary planets suggests that planetary formation processes can be highly adaptable and robust in surprisingly diverse environments. Their formation and evolution may differ significantly from planets in single-star systems, offering new insights into the intricacies of planetary formation processes under different physical conditions. The study of circumbinary planets opens up avenues for research on planetary migration, stability, and habitability in systems more complex than our own.

The study of exoplanets is a dynamic and rapidly evolving field. Each new discovery challenges our existing models and expands our understanding of the incredible diversity of planetary systems in the universe. As technology continues to improve, we can expect to discover even more unusual and intriguing types of exoplanets, expanding the horizons of our knowledge and pushing the boundaries of our imagination. The quest to understand exoplanets is not only a scientific endeavor but a journey of discovery that inspires us to contemplate our place in the vast cosmos and the potential for life beyond Earth. The ongoing research on exoplanets provides compelling evidence for the extraordinary diversity of planetary systems and the possibility of life elsewhere in the universe, further stimulating our curiosity and fueling our exploration of the cosmos.

Habitability of Exoplanets The Search for Life Beyond Earth

The discovery of thousands of exoplanets has profoundly altered our understanding of planetary systems, shifting our focus from a solar system-centric view to a broader cosmic perspective. While the sheer number of exoplanets is astonishing, the search for life beyond Earth hinges on identifying those with conditions conducive to life as we know it – a concept known as habitability. This quest involves carefully evaluating several key factors.

One crucial factor is a planet's size and mass. Planets that are too small, like Mercury, might lack sufficient gravity to retain a substantial atmosphere, leaving their surfaces exposed to harmful radiation. Conversely, planets that are too massive, like gas giants, possess crushing atmospheric pressures and temperatures, making them inhospitable. The "Goldilocks zone," a term often used in the context of habitability, represents the region around a star where the temperature is just right for liquid water to exist on the surface of a planet. This isn't a rigidly defined zone; it depends heavily on the star's luminosity and the planet's atmospheric composition. A planet slightly outside the traditionally defined habitable zone could still possess liquid water if its atmosphere contains sufficient greenhouse gasses to trap heat, warming the surface. Conversely, a planet within the habitable zone could still be frozen if its atmosphere is too thin or lacking in greenhouse gasses.

The composition of a planet's atmosphere is another critical determinant of habitability. The presence of certain gases can significantly influence a planet's temperature and chemistry. For example, the presence of abundant greenhouse gases like carbon dioxide, methane, and water vapor can trap heat, leading to a warmer surface temperature, even if the planet is relatively far from its star. Conversely, the absence of such gases could result in a frigid, uninhabitable environment.

Furthermore, the presence or absence of certain molecules can indicate the potential for biological processes. For example, the detection of oxygen in a planet's atmosphere could signify photosynthetic life, although this is not necessarily conclusive, as other non-biological processes could also generate oxygen. The presence of other biosignatures, such as methane, while often associated with life, needs to be carefully analyzed as geological processes can also produce it.

The detection and analysis of atmospheric components require sophisticated techniques. Spectroscopy, the study of how matter interacts with light, is crucial. By analyzing the spectrum of light passing through a planet's atmosphere, astronomers can identify the chemical fingerprints of various gases. However, this is a challenging task, requiring high- precision instruments and sophisticated data analysis techniques. Currently, our capabilities are limited to detecting relatively abundant gases in the atmospheres of large exoplanets, hindering the detection of subtle biosignatures in smaller, potentially habitable worlds. Future advancements in telescope technology, like the Extremely Large Telescope (ELT) and the James Webb Space Telescope (JWST), will be pivotal in improving our ability to characterize the atmospheres of smaller exoplanets and detect fainter spectral signatures.

Besides atmospheric composition, a planet's distance from its star, its rotation rate, and its axial tilt are crucial for determining habitability. A planet's distance determines the amount of stellar radiation it receives, which in turn affects its surface temperature. The rotation rate influences the length of the day and night cycles, which affect temperature variations and atmospheric circulation. A planet's axial tilt determines the seasons, influencing climate patterns.

Extreme axial tilts can lead to dramatic seasonal variations, potentially making the planet inhospitable. For example, Uranus, with its extreme axial tilt, experiences vastly different seasonal conditions.

The presence of a magnetic field also plays a critical role. A strong magnetic field can shield a planet's atmosphere from the harmful effects of stellar wind and cosmic rays, protecting it from erosion and potentially preserving the conditions necessary for life. Earth's magnetic field is a testament to the significance of this protective mechanism, deflecting charged particles from the Sun and preventing atmospheric stripping. The absence of a magnetic field could lead to the gradual loss of a planet's atmosphere over time.

Moreover, the presence of plate tectonics can have a profound influence on habitability. Plate tectonics plays a vital role in regulating the planet's climate through carbon cycling, influencing the concentration of greenhouse gases in the atmosphere, and thus, the overall temperature. The recycling of materials through plate tectonics also contributes to the long-term stability of the planet's surface environment and potentially its habitability.

The search for habitable exoplanets is a challenging but essential endeavor. It requires a multidisciplinary approach, combining expertise in astronomy, astrophysics, planetary science, and even biology. The development of advanced observational techniques, innovative data analysis methods, and sophisticated computer models is critical to unlocking the secrets of these distant worlds and identifying the factors that contribute to their habitability.

Currently, the most promising candidates for habitable exoplanets are super-Earths located within the habitable zone of their stars. These planets are larger than Earth but smaller than Neptune, and their composition could range from rocky worlds with substantial atmospheres to planets dominated by water. However, determining their actual habitability requires detailed characterization of their atmospheres, surface conditions, and internal structures.

The study of exoplanets is a dynamic and rapidly evolving field. Each new discovery and advancement in technology brings us closer to answering the fundamental question of whether life exists beyond Earth. As our observational capabilities improve, and our understanding of planetary formation and evolution deepens, we can expect to identify more and more promising candidates for potentially habitable exoplanets, potentially leading to the detection of biosignatures indicating the presence of extraterrestrial life. The quest for habitable exoplanets is not just a scientific pursuit but a journey of discovery that fuels our curiosity and expands our understanding of our place in the universe. It is a testament to human ingenuity and our unwavering desire to explore the unknown. The ultimate discovery of extraterrestrial life would undoubtedly be one of the most significant events in human history, fundamentally altering our perspective and enriching our understanding of the universe. Until then, the relentless search continues, driven by the unwavering belief that we are not alone.

Notable Exoplanet Discoveries and Their Significance

The sheer number of confirmed exoplanets – exceeding five thousand – is staggering, a testament to the relentless advancements in observational techniques and data analysis. However, simply knowing *that* exoplanets exist is only half the battle. The truly groundbreaking discoveries lie in the specific characteristics of these planets, revealing surprising diversity and challenging our preconceived notions about planetary systems. Among the notable discoveries are planets that push the boundaries of our understanding of planetary formation and evolution, those that reside within the habitable zones of their stars, and others that present unique atmospheric compositions hinting at potentially habitable conditions.

One of the early milestones in exoplanet discovery was the confirmation of 51 Pegasi b in 1995. This planet, a "hot Jupiter," orbits its star much closer than Mercury orbits our Sun. Its discovery was revolutionary because it shattered the then-prevailing assumption that gas giants could only form far from their stars, challenging the prevailing model of planetary formation within our own Solar System. The existence of hot Jupiters, massive gas giants orbiting incredibly close to their stars, forced a re-evaluation of planetary migration theories, suggesting that gravitational interactions with other planets or the protoplanetary disk could lead to significant orbital changes. This discovery highlighted the surprising diversity of planetary systems and opened the door to a whole new realm of theoretical exploration in planetary science.

Following the discovery of 51 Pegasi b, a flurry of hot Jupiter discoveries followed, many detected through the radial velocity method, which measures the slight wobble in a star's motion caused by the gravitational tug of an orbiting planet. While hot Jupiters are not typically considered habitable (due to their extreme temperatures and lack of a solid surface), their discovery was crucial for advancing the field and demonstrating the potential for finding more diverse and potentially habitable planets.

The Kepler mission, a space-based telescope launched in 2009, revolutionized exoplanet detection. Kepler employed the transit method, observing the slight dimming of a star's light as a planet passes in front of it. This technique allowed for the discovery of thousands of exoplanet candidates, many of which were smaller and less massive than previously detected planets. The sheer volume of data generated by Kepler was instrumental in identifying a range of planetary sizes and orbital periods, greatly expanding our understanding of the statistical distribution of exoplanets across different stellar systems.

Kepler's data revealed an unexpected abundance of "super- Earths," planets larger than Earth but smaller than Neptune. The nature of these super-Earths remains a subject of considerable research. Some may be rocky planets with significant atmospheres, while others might be "mini- Neptunes," planets primarily composed of gas and ice.

Determining the composition of these super-Earths is vital to assessing their potential habitability. The range of potential compositions and the existence of several within the habitable zone of their stars makes them prime candidates for future study.

Another significant breakthrough came with the discovery of planets in multiple-star systems. Previously, it was believed that planets might be less likely to form in such complex gravitational environments. However, discoveries of planets in binary and even trinary star systems demonstrated that planetary formation is possible under a much wider range of circumstances than initially thought, expanding the scope of where life could potentially emerge. The orbits of these planets, often complex and sometimes surprisingly stable, presented further challenges and opportunities for theorists trying to model planetary formation and evolution.

The discovery of TRAPPIST-1, a nearby ultra-cool dwarf star system hosting seven Earth-sized planets, in 2017, created immense excitement. Several of these planets reside within the star's habitable zone, though the nature of this "habitable zone" is unique due to the cooler nature of the dwarf star. The presence of liquid water would depend heavily on the planets' atmospheric composition and internal heat. The proximity of TRAPPIST-1 to Earth makes it a prime target for future atmospheric characterization using advanced telescopes like JWST. The possibility of multiple potentially habitable planets in a single system is incredibly significant, making TRAPPIST-1 one of the most important exoplanet systems ever discovered.

Furthermore, the discoveries of exoplanets orbiting different types of stars highlight the diversity of environments where planets can form. While much early research focused on Sun-like stars, discoveries of planets around red dwarfs, white dwarfs, and even neutron stars, significantly

broadened our perspective. Red dwarfs are the most common type of star in the galaxy, and the discovery of planets orbiting them presents the possibility of a large population of potentially habitable worlds. However, the challenges involved in assessing the habitability of planets orbiting red dwarfs include the effects of strong stellar flares and tidal locking – where one side of the planet always faces the star.

The detection of exoplanets orbiting white dwarfs, the remnants of Sun-like stars, presents another unique challenge. These planets are thought to have survived the star's red giant phase, a period of intense expansion that typically would destroy any nearby planets. The survival of these planets suggests a greater resilience of planetary systems than initially thought. Similarly, the discovery of a pulsar planet (a planet orbiting a rapidly rotating neutron star) was astonishing given the high-energy radiation environment of the pulsar. The existence of these planets underscores the complexity and adaptability of planetary systems.

Beyond specific planetary discoveries, the overall distribution of exoplanet properties across many systems has revolutionized our understanding. The prevalence of exoplanets, their diversity in size, mass, and orbital characteristics, and the discovery of planets around stars vastly different from our own has forced a significant revision of planetary formation models. These discoveries challenge simplistic models, highlighting the need for more nuanced and sophisticated models that incorporate multiple physical processes.

The significance of these discoveries extends beyond the realm of pure scientific understanding. The existence of potentially habitable exoplanets fuels our curiosity about the possibility of life beyond Earth and motivates further investment in observational technologies and theoretical models. The ongoing search for exoplanets is a compelling example of how scientific inquiry can expand our horizons and challenge our fundamental assumptions about our place in the cosmos.

The James Webb Space Telescope (JWST) promises to be a game-changer in exoplanet research. Its infrared capabilities allow for the detailed spectral analysis of exoplanet atmospheres, providing crucial insights into their composition, temperature, and potential habitability. JWST's high sensitivity will allow for the detection of fainter spectral signatures, providing more detailed information about smaller, potentially habitable planets. Its capabilities will allow scientists to identify and characterize biosignatures, molecular indicators that could indicate the presence of life. While we haven't yet found definitive proof of extraterrestrial life, JWST's observations hold immense promise for moving us closer to that monumental discovery. The data gathered by JWST will not only help us characterize the atmospheres of known exoplanets but will also significantly enhance our ability to find and analyze the atmospheres of new, potentially habitable planets.

The future of exoplanet research is bright. Future ground- based telescopes, such as the Extremely Large Telescope (ELT), will complement the space-based observations of JWST, providing higher resolution images and more detailed spectroscopic data. Continued advancements in observational techniques, data analysis methods, and theoretical modelling will allow for the identification and characterization of ever smaller and more distant planets, improving our ability to assess their potential habitability.

The ongoing quest to find and characterize exoplanets is not only a scientific endeavor but a journey of exploration and discovery, one that pushes the boundaries of human knowledge and potentially reveals one of the greatest discoveries in human history: the existence of life beyond Earth. The remarkable findings to date are only a prelude to the astonishing discoveries that undoubtedly await us in the years to come as our technological capabilities continue to advance. The universe is vast and teeming with secrets; the search for exoplanets is just beginning to unlock some of them.

Future Directions in Exoplanet Research

The discoveries detailed thus far represent a remarkable achievement, yet they are merely the first steps on a long and exciting journey. The future of exoplanet research promises even greater breakthroughs, fueled by ambitious new missions, technological advancements, and a growing understanding of planetary formation and evolution. The next generation of telescopes and observational techniques will allow astronomers to probe the atmospheres of exoplanets with unprecedented detail, revealing crucial information about their composition, climate, and potential habitability.

One of the most anticipated advancements is the continued operation and data analysis from the James Webb Space Telescope (JWST). While JWST's initial observations have already yielded impressive results, its full potential is still unfolding. JWST's infrared capabilities allow it to detect the faint heat signatures of exoplanets, even those orbiting relatively distant stars. This enables the spectroscopic analysis of exoplanet atmospheres, revealing the presence and abundance of various molecules. The detection of biosignatures – molecules that indicate the presence of life – is a primary goal of JWST's exoplanet research program.

While no definitive biosignatures have been detected yet, the ongoing and future analysis of JWST data holds tremendous promise.

The search for biosignatures requires extremely high precision and sensitivity. The subtle spectral signatures of gases like oxygen, methane, and water vapor, potentially produced by biological processes, must be distinguished from atmospheric components created by non-biological processes. This requires sophisticated data analysis techniques and detailed modeling of planetary atmospheres, taking into account factors like atmospheric pressure, temperature, and the composition of the host star. False positives are a significant concern, as atmospheric features that might initially appear promising could have purely geological or chemical origins. Rigorous scrutiny and multiple lines of evidence will be crucial in confirming any potential biosignature detection.

Beyond JWST, future ground-based telescopes are poised to revolutionize exoplanet research. The Extremely Large Telescope (ELT), currently under construction in Chile, will boast an unprecedented collecting area, providing significantly improved resolution and light-gathering capabilities. The ELT will be capable of directly imaging exoplanets, potentially capturing detailed images of their surfaces and clouds. Combined with advanced spectrographic instruments, the ELT will allow for more precise atmospheric characterization, even for relatively faint and distant exoplanets. This will extend our observation reach to planets which are more distant than those accessible by JWST and offer an independent verification of JWST's observations.

Furthermore, the development of advanced adaptive optics systems will further enhance the capabilities of both space- based and ground-based telescopes. Adaptive optics compensate for the blurring effect of Earth's atmosphere, significantly improving the resolution of ground-based observations. As these systems become more sophisticated, they will allow for sharper images and more precise spectroscopic measurements, pushing the limits of our ability to characterize distant exoplanets.

In addition to larger telescopes, novel observational techniques are continually being developed. For example, the use of coronagraphs, which block out the light of a star to reveal its fainter orbiting planets, is steadily improving.

These advances enable the direct imaging of exoplanets, offering a more direct means of characterizing their properties than indirect methods like the transit or radial velocity techniques. The ongoing development of space- based interferometers promises further advancement in direct imaging, offering even greater resolution and the potential to directly observe surface features of exoplanets.

The theoretical modeling of exoplanet atmospheres and planetary formation is also crucial for interpreting observational data. Sophisticated computer simulations are used to model the formation and evolution of planetary systems, considering factors like stellar evolution, protoplanetary disk dynamics, and planetary migration.

These models provide a framework for understanding the diverse range of exoplanets observed and predicting the properties of yet-to-be-discovered planets. The refinement of these models will be crucial to the interpretation of data from JWST and future telescopes.

The analysis of exoplanet atmospheres will require significant advancements in spectroscopic techniques and data analysis methods. The development of more sophisticated algorithms and machine-learning techniques will be essential for processing the vast amount of data generated by future telescopes. These techniques will aid in identifying subtle spectral features and separating them from noise, enabling more accurate determination of atmospheric composition and the potential presence of biosignatures.

Beyond atmospheric characterization, future research will focus on determining the internal structure and composition of exoplanets. This will involve combining observations with theoretical models to infer the presence and abundance of different layers within the planet, from the core to the atmosphere. Understanding the internal structure of an exoplanet is crucial for determining its thermal evolution and potential habitability. This may require novel techniques and analysis combining seismological measurements with other data.

The future of exoplanet research also encompasses the search for planets around different types of stars. While much research has focused on Sun-like stars, the potential for finding habitable planets around red dwarfs, brown dwarfs, and even white dwarfs remains a significant area of investigation. Each type of star presents unique challenges and opportunities for planetary formation and habitability. Red dwarfs, for instance, pose challenges due to the intense stellar flares and tidal locking, but they also represent a large portion of the galaxy's stars, thus potentially supporting a significant number of planetary systems. Understanding the prevalence and characteristics of planets around these varied stars is essential for a complete understanding of planetary systems across the galaxy.

Finally, the search for exoplanets is intrinsically linked to the search for extraterrestrial life. While the detection of biosignatures would be a monumental discovery, the absence of them doesn't necessarily rule out the possibility of life.

Future research will likely focus on developing more sensitive methods for detecting life beyond our planet, including the search for technosignatures – evidence of advanced technological civilizations. The search for extraterrestrial life is an inherently interdisciplinary endeavor, requiring the collaboration of astronomers, biologists, chemists, and others. The exciting discoveries to come will reshape our understanding of life and our place in the universe.

In conclusion, the future of exoplanet research is a dynamic and rapidly evolving field. The advancements in observational technology, data analysis, and theoretical modeling promise an era of unprecedented discoveries. The coming decades will likely reveal a wealth of information about exoplanet atmospheres, internal structures, and the potential for life beyond Earth. The journey to understand the universe's diversity of planetary systems and the possibility of life beyond our own world is a testament to human curiosity and the power of scientific inquiry. This quest is not just about scientific advancement; it is a journey of exploration that resonates deeply with our innate desire to discover our place within the vast cosmos.

Evidence for the Big Bang Theory

The remarkable progress in understanding the universe's evolution, from the formation of exoplanets to the vast expanse of interstellar space, leads us to one of the most profound and widely accepted theories in modern cosmology: the Big Bang theory. This theory proposes that the universe originated from an extremely hot, dense state approximately 13.8 billion years ago and has been expanding and cooling ever since. While we can't directly observe the very beginning of the universe, a wealth of observational evidence strongly supports the Big Bang model, painting a compelling picture of our cosmic origins.

One of the most compelling pieces of evidence is the cosmic microwave background radiation (CMB). Discovered accidentally in 1964 by Arno Penzias and Robert Wilson, the CMB is a faint afterglow of the Big Bang, a nearly uniform bath of microwave radiation permeating the entire universe. This radiation is incredibly uniform, with a temperature of about 2.7 Kelvin, a mere three degrees above absolute zero. This remarkable uniformity reflects the conditions of the early universe, when it was extremely hot and dense. The slight temperature variations in the CMB, only about one part in 100,000, are crucial. These tiny fluctuations represent the seeds of the large-scale structures we observe today – galaxies, galaxy clusters, and superclusters – providing a direct link between the early universe and the cosmos we see around us. The exquisite detail captured by missions like the Cosmic Background Explorer (COBE) and the Wilkinson Microwave Anisotropy Probe (WMAP), and more recently, the Planck satellite, has confirmed and refined our understanding of these fluctuations, offering precise measurements of cosmological parameters such as the age and composition of the universe. The CMB's near-perfect blackbody spectrum, matching the predicted radiation from a hot, dense plasma, provides strong evidence that the universe was once in this extreme state. Any deviation from this perfect blackbody spectrum would have cast serious doubt on the Big Bang theory. The exquisite match constitutes a powerful confirmation of the theory.

Further bolstering the Big Bang theory is the observed expansion of the universe. In the early 20th century, Edwin Hubble's observations revealed that distant galaxies are receding from us, and the farther away they are, the faster they are moving. This phenomenon, known as Hubble's Law, is elegantly explained by the Big Bang model. The universe is not merely expanding; it's expanding at an accelerating rate, a discovery that earned the 2011 Nobel Prize in Physics. This accelerated expansion is attributed to a mysterious force called dark energy, a component that makes up about 68% of the universe's energy density. The expansion itself implies that the universe must have been denser and hotter in the past, leading us back to the initial singularity – the incredibly hot and dense state from which the universe began. The precise measurements of the Hubble constant, a measure of the universe's expansion rate, continues to be refined through ongoing astronomical observations, further strengthening the Big Bang model. Discrepancies in the measured value of the Hubble constant from different observational methods remain a topic of ongoing research, potentially hinting at new physics yet to be fully understood.

The abundance of light elements in the universe also provides crucial support for the Big Bang theory. In the very early universe, conditions were hot enough for nuclear fusion to occur, producing light elements like hydrogen, helium, deuterium (a heavy isotope of hydrogen), and lithium. The Big Bang model predicts specific ratios of these elements based on the initial conditions of the universe. These predictions are remarkably consistent with the observed abundances of these elements in the universe. This agreement is a powerful testament to the Big Bang's ability to account for the fundamental building blocks of matter.

Any significant deviation between the predicted and observed abundances would seriously challenge the Big Bang model. The precision of these measurements continues to improve with advancements in observational techniques and theoretical modeling, reinforcing the consistency between theory and observation. The successful prediction of light element abundances represents a cornerstone of the Big Bang theory, demonstrating its ability to account for the composition of the universe on a fundamental level.

Beyond these three key pillars, other observations lend further credence to the Big Bang theory. For instance, the large-scale structure of the universe—the distribution of galaxies and galaxy clusters—closely matches the predictions of the Big Bang model, showcasing how the initial density fluctuations in the early universe grew through gravitational instability to form the cosmic web of galaxies we see today. Furthermore, the observed evolution of galaxies over cosmic time is consistent with the expectations of a universe that started in a hot, dense state and has been expanding and evolving ever since. Detailed observations of galaxy formation and evolution, using powerful telescopes across the electromagnetic spectrum, provide valuable insights into the universe's history. The redshift of distant galaxies, signifying their recession from us, provides further evidence for the universe's expansion. The cumulative effect of these many converging lines of evidence strengthens the Big Bang theory far beyond any single piece of observational data.

However, it's crucial to acknowledge that the Big Bang theory does not explain everything. For example, it doesn't address the very beginning of the universe or the nature of dark matter and dark energy, which together constitute the vast majority of the universe's content. These are significant unknowns, motivating ongoing research and stimulating the development of new theoretical frameworks to address these open questions. The mystery of dark matter, which interacts gravitationally but does not emit or absorb light, remains one of the most compelling puzzles in modern cosmology.

Similarly, dark energy, the force driving the accelerated expansion of the universe, is an enigma that continues to challenge our understanding of fundamental physics. These unresolved aspects of the Big Bang theory highlight the ongoing nature of scientific inquiry and emphasize the need for further exploration and experimentation.

Despite these unanswered questions, the overwhelming evidence strongly supports the Big Bang as the best available explanation for the origin and evolution of the universe. The CMB, the expansion of the universe, the abundance of light elements, and the large-scale structure of the cosmos all converge to point towards a universe that began in a hot, dense state and has been evolving ever since. The ongoing research, driven by the desire to better understand the universe's beginnings and its ultimate fate, continues to refine and extend our knowledge, pushing the boundaries of our understanding of the cosmos. Each new observation, each new refinement of cosmological models, strengthens the foundational aspects of the Big Bang theory while simultaneously unveiling new mysteries that beckon further exploration. The journey to fully understand the universe is a long and intricate one, but the Big Bang theory provides a robust and well-supported framework upon which to build our understanding of the cosmos. The pursuit of knowledge in this field is not merely an exercise in scientific curiosity;

it's a quest to unravel the story of our existence, our place in the vast expanse of spacetime.

The Inflationary Epoch and the Early Universe

The Big Bang theory, while remarkably successful in explaining the universe's evolution from a fraction of a second after its inception, encounters certain challenges when we attempt to extrapolate it back to the very beginning. One of these is the "horizon problem," which relates to the remarkable uniformity of the cosmic microwave background (CMB) radiation. The CMB is incredibly uniform across the entire observable universe, exhibiting only tiny temperature fluctuations. However, regions of the CMB that appear uniform today were causally disconnected in the early universe, meaning that light would not have had enough time to travel between them since the Big Bang. This implies that these regions should have different temperatures, contradicting the observed uniformity. How could these vastly separated regions have reached thermal equilibrium before the universe became transparent to radiation? This apparent paradox posed a significant challenge to the standard Big Bang model.

Another issue is the "flatness problem." The geometry of the universe, whether it's flat, spherical, or hyperbolic, is determined by its density. A flat universe has a critical density; a universe with a density greater than this is closed and spherical, while a universe with a lower density is open and hyperbolic. Observations suggest our universe is remarkably close to flat. The problem is that, even a tiny deviation from the critical density in the very early universe would have been amplified over cosmic time, leading to a significantly curved universe today. The fact that our universe is so close to flat suggests a fine-tuning that is difficult to explain within the standard Big Bang framework.

This near-perfect flatness also seems suspiciously improbable, hinting at a deeper underlying process.

Yet another puzzle is the "monopole problem." Grand unified theories (GUTs), which attempt to unify the fundamental forces of nature at extremely high energies, predict the existence of magnetic monopoles – hypothetical particles with only one magnetic pole. These monopoles should have been produced in vast numbers in the very early universe. However, we have yet to detect any, posing a significant challenge to GUTs and the standard Big Bang model. The absence of these predicted particles, despite their expected abundance, demands explanation.

To address these problems, the inflationary epoch theory was proposed. This theory postulates a period of extremely rapid exponential expansion in the very early universe, occurring within a tiny fraction of a second after the Big Bang. During inflation, the universe expanded at an unimaginably fast rate, far exceeding the expansion rate predicted by the standard Big Bang model. This rapid expansion, driven by a hypothetical energy field called the inflaton field, has profound implications for resolving the cosmological problems described above.

How does inflation solve the horizon problem? The key is that during inflation, causally connected regions expanded enormously. Regions that were once close enough to interact thermally during the very early universe were stretched far apart during inflation. Before inflation, these regions were in thermal equilibrium, and inflation simply stretched them apart while maintaining their uniform temperature.

Therefore, the observed uniformity of the CMB is not a coincidence but a consequence of inflation stretching out an initially small, causally connected region into the vast universe we observe today. It's like taking a small patch of a perfectly smooth surface and stretching it enormously; even though the resulting area is vast, the uniformity remains.

Inflation also provides a solution to the flatness problem. Imagine the universe as a balloon. If the balloon is nearly flat, it will appear increasingly flat as it expands. Inflationary expansion is so rapid that it stretches out any initial curvature, making the universe effectively flat, regardless of its initial geometry. The rapid expansion "smooths out" any initial curvature, resulting in the almost perfectly flat universe we observe. It's analogous to stretching a slightly curved piece of fabric; as it expands, the curvature becomes increasingly less noticeable.

Finally, inflation solves the monopole problem. While GUTs predict the production of magnetic monopoles, inflation dilutes their density to such an extent that their abundance becomes negligible. The rapid expansion effectively "dilutes" the monopoles, spreading them so thinly throughout space that they become practically undetectable. This provides a natural explanation for the lack of observed monopoles.

It's important to note that the inflationary theory is not without its own challenges and uncertainties. The nature of the inflaton field, the specific mechanism driving inflation, and the precise details of the inflationary epoch remain open questions. However, the ability of inflation to elegantly address some of the most pressing problems of the standard Big Bang model makes it a compelling and influential addition to our understanding of the early universe.

The evidence for inflation is indirect but increasingly persuasive. The extremely high degree of homogeneity in the CMB, the near-flatness of the universe, and the absence of magnetic monopoles all support the inflationary scenario.

Further, inflation makes predictions about the spectrum of density fluctuations in the early universe, which are reflected in the subtle temperature anisotropies observed in the CMB. The precise measurements of these anisotropies by the Planck satellite, for instance, have shown remarkable agreement with the predictions of inflationary models, adding substantial weight to the theory. These observations don't provide a direct "image" of inflation itself, but the statistical properties of the fluctuations show the fingerprints of inflation, implying a period of incredibly rapid expansion in the very early universe.

Furthermore, different models of inflation predict slightly different features in the CMB, and future observations may allow us to discriminate between them. Ongoing research continues to refine our understanding of inflation and test its predictions. The search for observational signatures of inflation is a forefront area in modern cosmology, pushing the boundaries of our understanding of the universe's infancy. The precision of cosmological observations is constantly improving, allowing us to probe ever deeper into the conditions of the early universe and test the validity of inflationary theories with increased accuracy.

In summary, while the Big Bang theory describes the universe's evolution from a fraction of a second onward, the inflationary epoch theory adds a crucial layer to our understanding of the very earliest moments. Inflation provides a natural and elegant solution to the horizon, flatness, and monopole problems of the standard Big Bang model, explaining the remarkable uniformity of the universe and its near-perfect flatness. While much remains to be discovered about the details of inflation, the accumulating evidence strongly suggests that it played a vital role in shaping the universe we observe today, leaving its distinctive mark on the fabric of spacetime. The quest to understand inflation remains a central challenge and an exciting area of research in contemporary cosmology, pushing the boundaries of our theoretical and observational capabilities. The success in accommodating inflation within the broader Big Bang framework highlights the power of scientific investigation and the evolving nature of our understanding of the universe. The journey to completely comprehend the cosmos, its beginning, and its ultimate destiny is a long and challenging endeavor, but the constant refinement and extension of our theories, driven by rigorous observations and theoretical breakthroughs, steadily illuminates the path forward.

The Formation of Galaxies and Stars

The universe, having emerged from the inflationary epoch, was far from the familiar tapestry of stars and galaxies we see today. It was a remarkably uniform sea of hot, dense plasma, a nearly perfect soup of protons, neutrons, electrons, and photons. However, this uniformity was not absolute.

Tiny ripples, subtle fluctuations in density, existed within this primordial plasma. These minuscule variations, far smaller than a single part in a million, were the seeds from which the grand structures of the universe – galaxies and stars – would eventually grow. These fluctuations, predicted by inflation and later confirmed by observations of the cosmic microwave background, are crucial to understanding the subsequent formation of cosmic structures. They weren't random noise; their subtle variations in amplitude and scale held the blueprint of the universe's future.

The origin of these density fluctuations remains a subject of active research, but the leading theory posits that quantum fluctuations during inflation were stretched to cosmic scales during the period of rapid expansion. Imagine the universe at this stage as an incredibly smooth, but not perfectly uniform, surface. Quantum fluctuations, normally confined to minuscule scales, were magnified by the inflationary expansion, creating variations in density across vast regions of space. These variations, while incredibly small initially, were the crucial initial conditions for the formation of the first stars and galaxies. The expansion itself amplified these tiny seeds into the larger structures we see today.

As the universe continued to expand and cool, the plasma gradually transitioned from an opaque to a transparent state. This transition, known as recombination, occurred around

380,000 years after the Big Bang. At this point, the energy levels dropped sufficiently for protons and electrons to combine and form neutral hydrogen atoms. This event is of paramount importance because it marks the moment when the universe became transparent to light. The photons that were previously scattering off the charged particles could now travel freely, creating the cosmic microwave background radiation (CMB) that we observe today.

The CMB carries within it a wealth of information about the early universe, including the initial density fluctuations that served as the seeds for structure formation. The CMB is not perfectly uniform; tiny temperature variations correspond to slight differences in density. Regions that were slightly denser attracted more matter through gravitational attraction, acting as gravitational wells. These regions continued to accumulate more matter over time, creating ever-larger clumps in a process known as gravitational instability.

This process of gravitational collapse was not instantaneous. It was a slow, gradual process spanning millions and billions of years. The denser regions, with slightly higher-than- average density, had a stronger gravitational pull. This caused them to attract more and more surrounding matter, accumulating mass and becoming even denser. This is a positive feedback loop; more mass attracts more mass, leading to an ever-increasing density in those regions. It's a bit like a snowball effect, where a small initial snowball rolls down a hill, accumulating more and more snow as it goes.

The slight initial density difference serves as the seed for a much larger mass concentration in the future.

Meanwhile, in the regions with lower-than-average density, the matter was less concentrated and so the gravitational pull was weaker. These regions expanded more rapidly than their denser counterparts, further enhancing the contrast between the underdense and overdense regions. This process of gravitational clustering is a fundamental mechanism in the formation of large-scale structures in the universe. Over immense stretches of time, these initially subtle density variations evolved into the vast cosmic web we see today.

As these dense regions continued to collapse under their own gravity, they fragmented into smaller clumps. These clumps were the precursors of galaxies and galaxy clusters. The process wasn't uniform; some regions collapsed faster than others, depending on their initial density and the distribution of surrounding matter. Within these proto-galaxies, the density continued to increase until the gravitational forces became strong enough to trigger the formation of the first stars.

The formation of the first stars was a pivotal event in the history of the universe. These Population III stars, as they are called, were vastly different from the stars we observe today. They were much larger, more massive, and hotter, primarily composed of hydrogen and helium, the only elements produced in significant quantities during the Big Bang. The lack of heavier elements, crucial for stellar processes in stars today, played a significant role in their characteristics and lifecycles.

These colossal stars lived short, dramatic lives, burning through their fuel rapidly. When they died, they exploded as supernovae, scattering heavier elements produced during their short lifecycles into the surrounding interstellar medium. These elements, forged in the hearts of these first stars, were crucial for the formation of subsequent generations of stars.

The subsequent generations of stars, known as Population II and Population I stars, inherited these heavier elements.

Population II stars, formed slightly later, already contained some heavier elements, reflecting the enrichment of the interstellar medium by the first-generation stars. Population I stars, including our Sun, are relatively rich in heavier elements, demonstrating the continuous enrichment of the interstellar medium over cosmic time. The composition of stars reflects the history of star formation and stellar nucleosynthesis, providing a direct link to the universe's past.

The distribution of galaxies in the universe is not random. They are arranged in a vast cosmic web, a complex network of filaments, clusters, and voids. This large-scale structure, reflecting the initial density fluctuations, provides further evidence for the gravitational instability theory. The filaments and clusters are regions where matter accumulated over time, while the voids are regions where the density remained relatively low. The scale and distribution of this cosmic web provide crucial insights into the initial conditions of the universe and the processes of structure formation.

Galaxies themselves are complex and dynamic systems, with their formation and evolution shaped by a multitude of factors. Gravitational interactions between galaxies, mergers, and the interplay between stars, gas, and dark matter all play crucial roles. Simulations of galaxy formation, using sophisticated computational tools, help us to understand this complexity and to test theoretical models against observational data. However, the detailed processes governing galaxy formation and evolution remain an area of intense research, and there is much we still don't understand.

In summary, the formation of galaxies and stars is a complex process that spans billions of years. It begins with the tiny density fluctuations in the early universe, amplified by gravity and inflation. These fluctuations grow into the large- scale structures we observe today, culminating in the formation of galaxies and, within them, stars. The detailed processes governing this formation are still being actively researched, but the overall picture is now reasonably well- understood. The journey from the nearly uniform universe following inflation to the rich and complex tapestry of stars and galaxies we see today is a testament to the power of gravity and the remarkable consequences of even tiny initial variations. The story continues to be refined with each new observation and theoretical advance, pushing the boundaries of our understanding of the universe's grand history and evolution.

Dark Matter and Dark Energy

The story of the universe's evolution from a hot, dense plasma to the structured cosmos we observe today is far from complete. While the formation of galaxies and stars from initial density fluctuations provides a compelling narrative, a significant piece of the puzzle remains missing: the overwhelming majority of the universe's mass-energy budget is unaccounted for. This missing mass-energy is attributed to two enigmatic components: dark matter and dark energy.

Dark matter, despite its name, is not a void or absence of matter; it's a mysterious substance that interacts gravitationally with ordinary matter but doesn't emit, absorb, or reflect light, making it virtually invisible to our telescopes. Its existence is inferred through its gravitational effects on visible matter, galaxies, and galaxy clusters. For example, the rotation curves of galaxies – the speed at which stars orbit the galactic center – don't match predictions based solely on the visible matter. Stars in the outer regions of galaxies orbit much faster than they should if only the visible matter contributed to the galaxy's gravitational pull. This discrepancy suggests the presence of a significant amount of unseen matter, providing extra gravitational force to keep the stars from flying off into intergalactic space. This "extra" gravity is attributed to dark matter, effectively acting as the invisible glue holding galaxies together.

Further evidence for dark matter comes from observations of galaxy clusters. These immense conglomerations of galaxies contain vast amounts of hot gas, emitting X-rays that are detectable by our telescopes. However, the gravitational potential of these clusters, inferred from the motion of galaxies within them, is much greater than can be explained by the visible matter and the hot gas alone. Again, the missing gravitational pull points to a significant unseen component – dark matter. Gravitational lensing, where light from distant galaxies is bent by the gravity of intervening matter, also provides compelling evidence for dark matter. The degree of lensing observed suggests the presence of much more mass than is visible.

The nature of dark matter remains one of the biggest mysteries in modern astrophysics. While we know it interacts gravitationally, its fundamental properties remain unknown. Various theoretical candidates have been proposed, ranging from weakly interacting massive particles (WIMPs) to axions, but conclusive experimental verification is still elusive. Experiments deep underground, shielded from cosmic rays, are designed to detect WIMPs by their extremely rare interactions with ordinary matter. Other experiments focus on detecting axions, extremely light particles that might constitute a significant fraction of dark matter. The search for dark matter is a high-priority area of research, and the eventual identification of its fundamental constituents will revolutionize our understanding of the universe.

While dark matter accounts for a significant portion of the universe's missing mass, dark energy represents an even more profound mystery. Observations of distant supernovae, exploding stars used as standard candles to measure cosmic distances, revealed a startling fact: the expansion of the universe is accelerating. This acceleration implies the existence of a repulsive force, counteracting gravity's attractive pull, and pushing the galaxies apart at an ever- increasing rate. This mysterious force is attributed to dark energy, a component with an anti-gravitational effect, driving the accelerating expansion of the cosmos.

The discovery of the universe's accelerating expansion came as a complete surprise. Most cosmologists had expected the expansion to slow down due to the attractive force of gravity. The unexpected discovery of this acceleration, awarded the 2011 Nobel Prize in Physics, fundamentally changed our understanding of the universe's evolution. The acceleration suggests that dark energy constitutes about 68% of the universe's total energy density, far surpassing the combined contributions of dark matter (about 27%) and ordinary matter (about 5%).

Unlike dark matter, whose interaction is primarily gravitational, dark energy interacts differently, exhibiting a repulsive gravitational effect. Its nature remains deeply enigmatic, and several theoretical explanations have been proposed, including the cosmological constant, a constant energy density inherent in the fabric of spacetime, and quintessence, a dynamical energy field whose density varies over time and space. Both theories offer intriguing possibilities but are limited by our current understanding of fundamental physics. The cosmological constant, proposed by Einstein himself, and later rejected, is now considered a viable candidate, but its extraordinarily small value remains unexplained. Quintessence, on the other hand, offers the potential for a more dynamic universe, where the properties of dark energy can evolve over time. The ongoing study of dark energy, through precise measurements of the expansion rate of the universe, surveys of large-scale structures, and further investigations into fundamental physics, are crucial for unveiling the nature of this enigmatic component.

The implications of dark matter and dark energy are profound, extending beyond simply filling the missing mass- energy budget. They fundamentally reshape our understanding of the universe's evolution, composition, and ultimate fate. The presence of dark energy, for instance, implies that the universe's expansion will continue indefinitely, ultimately leading to a cold, sparsely populated universe, where galaxies are increasingly separated and interaction between them is minimal. This "Big Freeze" scenario contrasts sharply with previous models that predicted a potential re-collapse of the universe.

The study of dark matter and dark energy is at the forefront of modern astrophysics and cosmology. Sophisticated telescopes, such as the Hubble Space Telescope and the upcoming James Webb Space Telescope, are enabling unprecedented observations of the universe's large-scale structure, helping refine our models of dark matter and dark energy. Ground-based telescopes, such as those at the Very Large Telescope in Chile, provide further observational data, crucial for constraining theoretical models and advancing our understanding. In parallel, particle physicists are designing and building increasingly sophisticated experiments to probe the fundamental nature of dark matter particles in hopes of detecting them directly.

The quest to understand these enigmatic components is not merely an academic pursuit; it represents a fundamental shift in our understanding of the physical universe and its governing principles. The discovery of dark matter and dark energy has challenged our existing models and has opened up new avenues of research, pushing the boundaries of theoretical physics and experimental technology. The answers to these profound questions remain elusive, but the pursuit itself promises a wealth of new discoveries and a deeper understanding of the universe's enigmatic nature. The next decades will likely witness significant breakthroughs in our understanding of dark matter and dark energy, potentially revolutionizing our perception of the cosmos and our place within it. The journey of understanding the universe is far from over; rather, it has just entered a new and exciting chapter, fueled by the tantalizing mysteries of dark matter and dark energy. The challenge is enormous, but the potential rewards – a deeper understanding of the universe's very fabric – are immeasurable.

The Fate of the Universe

The profound mysteries of dark matter and dark energy, as discussed previously, don't merely fill gaps in our understanding of the universe's composition; they fundamentally reshape our predictions for its ultimate fate. For decades, the prevailing cosmological model envisioned a universe whose expansion, initiated by the Big Bang, would eventually slow down and potentially even reverse, leading to a "Big Crunch"—a catastrophic collapse back into a singularity. This scenario, however, is now largely superseded by observations indicating an accelerating expansion, driven by the repulsive force of dark energy. This leads us to contemplate a different, and perhaps more unsettling, cosmic future.

The most widely accepted scenario for the universe's ultimate fate, given the current evidence for dark energy's dominance, is the "Big Freeze," also known as the "heat death" of the universe. In this scenario, the continued acceleration of the expansion will relentlessly push galaxies further and further apart. The distances between them will become so vast that the light from distant galaxies will eventually become undetectable, effectively erasing them from our observable universe. This isn't merely a matter of galaxies moving away; the expansion itself is stretching space-time, causing the fabric of the universe to expand and dilute the energy density.

Over immense stretches of cosmic time, the expansion will continue to accelerate. The increasing separation between galaxies will eventually lead to a state of extreme isolation. Stars will continue to burn and die, eventually leaving behind stellar remnants like white dwarfs, neutron stars, and black holes. As the universe expands, these objects will become increasingly isolated, with no possibility of interaction or merging. The density of matter and energy will continue to decrease, approaching absolute zero. The universe will become a cold, dark, and essentially empty expanse, a stark contrast to the dynamic and vibrant universe we observe today.

The Big Freeze isn't simply a cessation of activity; it's a gradual fading into an increasingly desolate and homogeneous state. The second law of thermodynamics, which dictates the increase of entropy—the measure of disorder in a system—is a key player in this scenario. As the universe expands, its entropy increases, leading to a gradual homogenization of energy and matter. This means that energy will become increasingly dispersed and less usable, making it impossible for complex structures like stars and galaxies to form.

While the Big Freeze is the most plausible scenario given our current understanding, it's crucial to acknowledge the inherent uncertainties. Our knowledge of dark energy is far from complete. Its properties, its origin, and its ultimate behavior remain significant mysteries. The possibility that the properties of dark energy might change over time cannot be ruled out. If, for instance, dark energy's repulsive force were to weaken or even disappear, the expansion of the universe could slow down, and potentially even reverse, leading to a Big Crunch after all.

A less likely, but theoretically possible, alternative to the Big Freeze is the "Big Rip." This scenario hinges on the specific nature of dark energy. If dark energy's density continues to increase over time, it could eventually overcome the gravitational forces holding together galaxies, stars, planets, and even atoms. In the extreme version of this scenario, the accelerating expansion becomes so violent that it tears apart all structures in the universe, ripping them asunder atom by atom. This would represent a truly catastrophic end to the universe, far more dramatic than the gradual cooling and isolation of the Big Freeze.

The contrasting scenarios—Big Freeze and Big Rip—highlight the profound influence of dark energy on the universe's ultimate fate. The precise nature of dark energy and its future behavior will determine which of these scenarios, or perhaps another entirely unforeseen outcome, awaits the universe. The possibility of a Big Rip, though seemingly extreme, underscores the importance of further research into the nature of dark energy. This research needs to go beyond simply measuring its current effects; it requires a deeper understanding of its fundamental properties and its potential evolution over cosmic timescales.

The uncertainties surrounding the universe's fate underscore the limits of our current cosmological models. While these models provide compelling frameworks for understanding the universe's evolution, they are fundamentally based on our current understanding of physics and the observed properties of dark energy and dark matter. As our observational capabilities improve and our theoretical understanding advances, our predictions about the universe's ultimate fate may well be refined or even revolutionized.

Our understanding of the universe is a work in progress. Every new observation, every refinement of our theoretical models, challenges and refines our understanding of its past, present, and future. The quest to understand the universe's ultimate fate is not simply an intellectual exercise; it is a journey into the very heart of existence, a search for answers that reach beyond the confines of our current understanding and challenge us to explore the limits of our knowledge.

The Big Freeze, the Big Crunch, the Big Rip—these scenarios are not simply narrative endings; they represent potential futures, each with profound implications for our understanding of the universe's evolution and its fundamental physical laws. The uncertainties inherent in these predictions, however, serve as a constant reminder of the vastness and mystery of the cosmos and the ongoing challenge of understanding its workings. The journey to decipher the universe's ultimate fate is a continuous exploration, an unending quest fueled by curiosity, innovation, and the unwavering human desire to comprehend the universe's deepest secrets.

Further complicating the picture is the possibility of unforeseen physical processes, unknown laws of physics, or even quantum effects that could significantly alter the universe's long-term evolution. The very fabric of space-time itself might undergo transformations beyond our current comprehension, leading to outcomes that defy our current cosmological models. This underscores the fact that our predictions about the universe's ultimate fate are contingent upon our current understanding, which is inherently incomplete.

The scientific method, with its iterative process of observation, hypothesis formulation, testing, and refinement, remains our best tool for navigating this vast ocean of uncertainty. By continually refining our observations and developing more sophisticated theoretical models, we can progressively refine our understanding of dark energy, dark matter, and their roles in shaping the universe's future. This ongoing investigation is not merely an academic exercise; it has profound philosophical implications for our understanding of our place in the universe and the nature of existence itself. The search for answers continues, pushing the boundaries of human knowledge and driving the advancement of scientific understanding for generations to come. The universe's fate remains a captivating enigma, a challenge to our intellect and a constant source of inspiration for our explorations. The quest to unravel this mystery is a testament to humanity's innate drive to understand its place in the vast and awe-inspiring cosmos.

The Formation of Black Holes

Having explored the universe's potential ultimate fates, driven largely by the enigmatic forces of dark matter and dark energy, we now turn our attention to some of the most fascinating and extreme objects within it: black holes. These cosmic vacuum cleaners, as they are often called, represent the ultimate triumph of gravity, regions of spacetime where gravity is so strong that nothing, not even light, can escape their grasp. But how do these enigmatic objects form? The answer, as with much in astrophysics, is complex and multifaceted, with several distinct pathways leading to the creation of these gravitational behemoths.

The most common path to black hole formation begins with the life cycle of a massive star. Stars are colossal spheres of plasma, held together by the delicate balance between the inward pull of gravity and the outward push of nuclear fusion reactions in their cores. These reactions, which convert hydrogen into helium and other heavier elements, generate immense amounts of energy, counteracting the crushing force of gravity. The size and mass of a star dictate the length and nature of its life cycle.

For stars many times more massive than our Sun—typically, those exceeding eight solar masses—this equilibrium is a temporary state. While their immense size allows for far more vigorous fusion reactions, these reactions consume the star's hydrogen fuel at a breathtaking rate. Their lifespan, measured in mere millions of years, is a fleeting moment compared to the billions of years our Sun has ahead of it.

When a massive star approaches the end of its hydrogen fuel supply, it enters a period of dramatic instability.

The core of the star, now primarily composed of helium and other heavier elements, begins to contract under its own gravity. This contraction triggers a series of further fusion reactions, involving successively heavier elements, like carbon, oxygen, neon, and silicon. Each of these stages is short-lived, punctuated by increasingly violent explosions and releases of energy. However, the star's core continues to contract, ultimately reaching a point where it can no longer sustain further fusion. At this critical juncture, the core's ability to generate outward pressure against gravity finally fails.

Gravity takes over decisively. The core collapses catastrophically, imploding upon itself at an incredible speed. This collapse releases an enormous amount of gravitational energy, triggering a supernova explosion—a cosmic event of unparalleled power. A supernova is so bright that it can briefly outshine an entire galaxy, and the immense energy released blasts the star's outer layers into space, seeding the interstellar medium with heavy elements forged in the star's core.

The fate of the core itself depends on its initial mass. If the core is relatively light—between 1.4 and 3 solar masses—it will form a neutron star, a fantastically dense object composed almost entirely of neutrons. These neutrons are crammed together incredibly tightly, creating an object with a density so high that a teaspoonful of neutron star material would weigh billions of tons on Earth.

However, if the stellar core is much heavier, exceeding approximately 3 solar masses, even the immense pressure of neutron degeneracy, which counteracts the core's gravitational collapse in less massive stars, is insufficient to prevent further collapse. Gravity continues its relentless march inward, compressing the core to an unimaginably small size, creating a singularity—a point of infinite density and zero volume. Surrounding the singularity is the event horizon, a boundary beyond which the gravitational pull is so intense that nothing, not even light, can escape. This is a black hole.

The formation of black holes, then, is a testament to gravity's overwhelming power. It's a dramatic, violent event that transforms a massive star into an object of unimaginable density and gravitational intensity. But the story doesn't end there. The mass of the black hole, formed from the collapsed core of a massive star, generally falls within a certain range, commonly referred to as stellar-mass black holes. These black holes can be many times the mass of the Sun, but their size is significantly less than the supermassive black holes found at the centers of galaxies.

This leads to the intriguing question of how supermassive black holes, often containing millions or even billions of solar masses, form. Several theories attempt to explain their origins, and the answer may not be a single process, but rather a combination of factors. One prominent theory suggests that supermassive black holes originate from the collapse of extremely massive gas clouds in the early universe. These clouds, far more massive than any single star, could collapse directly into a supermassive black hole without going through the supernova stage.

Another theory proposes a process of "seed" black holes. This hypothesis suggests that a smaller, stellar-mass black hole may form first, and through a process of accretion— grabbing and consuming surrounding matter and even merging with other black holes—it gradually grows into a supermassive black hole over millions or billions of years. This continuous feeding and merging is facilitated by the dense environment of the galactic core, where vast quantities of gas and dust provide abundant fuel for the growing black hole.

Evidence for these merging events is provided by gravitational waves, ripples in spacetime predicted by Einstein's theory of general relativity. These waves are generated by the violent collision of massive objects, such as black holes. The detection of gravitational waves from merging black holes, including some evidence of mergers involving supermassive black holes, has revolutionized our understanding of these extreme cosmic objects and provides strong support for the theory of seed black hole growth and mergers.

The formation of supermassive black holes remains an area of active research. While the accretion of surrounding matter is a critical factor in their growth, the exact mechanisms and initial conditions that lead to their formation are still being investigated. The study of these enigmatic objects requires sophisticated observational techniques, including powerful telescopes capable of probing the hearts of galaxies, and detailed theoretical models that grapple with the complexities of gravity at extreme scales.

As our understanding of black holes deepens, we gain further insight into the fundamental forces that shape the universe. The processes leading to their formation, from the catastrophic collapse of massive stars to the potential growth and mergers of smaller black holes, unveil the extreme conditions and events that occur within our universe. The study of black holes serves not only to understand these extreme objects themselves but also to further test and refine our understanding of gravity, spacetime, and the very fabric of the cosmos. The ongoing quest to understand black hole formation remains a captivating and vital area of astrophysical research, pushing the boundaries of our knowledge and deepening our appreciation of the universe's profound complexity. The mysteries surrounding black holes continue to drive us forward, fueling our intellectual curiosity and our relentless pursuit of knowledge. The continuing revelations promise to further enhance our understanding of the universe's dynamic and awe-inspiring evolution.

Properties of Black Holes Event Horizon Singularity and Gravity

Having established the formation pathways of both stellar- mass and supermassive black holes, we now delve into the fascinating and perplexing properties that define these cosmic entities. Understanding these properties is crucial to appreciating their profound impact on the universe and their role in shaping galactic evolution. Three key features stand out: the event horizon, the singularity, and the unparalleled gravitational influence exerted by black holes.

The event horizon acts as the black hole's boundary, a point of no return. Imagine throwing a ball into the air. Earth's gravity pulls it back down. However, if you were to throw it with sufficient velocity – escape velocity – it would overcome Earth's gravity and escape into space. Black holes are different. Their gravity is so immense that the escape velocity exceeds the speed of light. This means that once anything crosses the event horizon, it is inevitably drawn towards the black hole's center, regardless of its speed or direction. No information, not even light, can escape from within the event horizon. This makes observation of the singularity directly impossible, requiring indirect methods and theoretical models to understand its nature.

The concept of the event horizon is intrinsically linked to the curvature of spacetime. Einstein's theory of general relativity describes gravity not as a force, but as a curvature of spacetime caused by the presence of mass and energy.

Imagine a bowling ball placed on a stretched rubber sheet. The ball creates a dip, warping the sheet's surface. Similarly, massive objects warp spacetime. The more massive the object, the greater the curvature. A black hole's immense mass creates such an extreme curvature of spacetime that it forms a "well" from which nothing can climb out, the edge of this "well" being the event horizon. The closer you get to the black hole, the steeper the slope of spacetime, and the stronger the gravitational pull. This curvature isn't merely a visual analogy; it's a fundamental aspect of reality within Einstein's framework, a bending of the fabric of spacetime itself. The geometry of spacetime around a black hole is profoundly altered, making even concepts like time and space behave in unexpected ways.

The size of the event horizon, often referred to as the Schwarzschild radius, is directly proportional to the black hole's mass. A black hole with twice the mass will have an event horizon with twice the radius. This means that despite their reputation for being "points of infinite density," black holes do possess a physical size, albeit one determined by their gravity. This radius encapsulates a region of spacetime from which nothing can escape, creating the black hole's characteristic boundary and a crucial element for understanding their interactions with surrounding material.

The singularity is the theoretical point at the very center of a black hole, a region of infinite density and zero volume. Our current understanding of physics breaks down at the singularity. The laws of general relativity, which accurately describe gravity at most scales, become inapplicable when dealing with infinite densities. This indicates that a more complete theory of gravity, perhaps a quantum theory of gravity, is needed to fully comprehend the nature of the singularity. It's a region where the familiar laws of physics cease to function, a realm of extremes that challenges our understanding of the universe's fundamental workings. This is not simply a limitation of our current knowledge; it points towards the fundamental incompatibility of our theories of general relativity, which governs the very large, and quantum mechanics, which rules the very small. Bridging this gap remains one of the biggest challenges in modern theoretical physics.

The singularity is not a physical object in the conventional sense; it's a point where the known laws of physics cease to function. Imagine trying to describe the temperature at a point where the temperature is infinitely high – it becomes meaningless. Similarly, assigning a volume or density to a point of infinite density is conceptually problematic. It represents a breakdown of our current models and highlights the limitations of our understanding of the universe's most extreme environments. It necessitates the development of a new theoretical framework that can accommodate infinite densities and resolve the inherent paradoxes of our current physical laws when applied to such extreme conditions.

The gravitational pull of a black hole is, naturally, extraordinary. Its intensity is dictated by the black hole's mass and the proximity to the event horizon. The closer an object gets to the event horizon, the stronger the gravitational pull becomes, eventually reaching an insurmountable force. This immense gravity affects not only matter but also light itself, bending its path as it passes near a black hole. This effect, known as gravitational lensing, has been observed and verified, providing observational evidence to support Einstein's predictions about the curvature of spacetime. Gravitational lensing manifests as a distortion of the light from background objects, creating magnified and often multiple images of distant galaxies. This phenomenon acts as a cosmic magnifying glass, enhancing our ability to study distant parts of the universe.

Furthermore, the immense gravity of black holes plays a crucial role in galactic dynamics. Supermassive black holes, residing at the centers of most galaxies, act as gravitational anchors, influencing the motions of stars and gas clouds within their host galaxies. Their gravitational influence shapes the galactic structure, creating a gravitational well that keeps stars and gas orbiting around the central black hole. The relationship between black holes and their host galaxies is a dynamic one, involving feedback mechanisms that regulate the growth of both the galaxy and the black hole. Observations and simulations suggest that the mass of the central black hole is correlated with the mass of the galactic bulge, the central region of the galaxy composed of densely packed stars. This correlation hints at a co- evolutionary relationship between the central black hole and the galaxy itself, a subject of ongoing research and debate.

The gravitational effects of black holes extend far beyond their immediate vicinity. The gravitational waves generated by merging black holes, as mentioned earlier, provide a unique window into these extreme events. These ripples in spacetime, predicted by Einstein's general theory of relativity, are a testament to the profound impact of black holes on the fabric of the universe. The detection of gravitational waves has opened a new era in astronomy, allowing us to observe events that were previously invisible to conventional telescopes. It confirmed a fundamental prediction of Einstein's theory and provided a new means to study the most violent and energetic events in the cosmos.

In summary, the event horizon, singularity, and gravitational pull are defining characteristics of black holes. The event horizon is the point of no return, the boundary beyond which escape is impossible. The singularity is a region of infinite density at the center, where our current understanding of physics breaks down. And the immense gravity of black holes profoundly influences their surroundings, shaping galactic structures and generating gravitational waves that ripple throughout the universe. Continued research into black holes is essential not only to understand these extraordinary objects but also to deepen our fundamental understanding of gravity, spacetime, and the universe itself. The quest to unravel the mysteries of black holes is a testament to humanity's relentless pursuit of knowledge, driving advancements in theoretical physics, observational astronomy, and our comprehension of the cosmos's most enigmatic entities. The mysteries surrounding black holes continue to inspire and challenge us, pushing the boundaries of our scientific understanding and expanding our grasp of the universe's breathtaking complexity.

Observing Black Holes Indirect Evidence and Gravitational Waves

The invisibility of black holes, cloaked as they are by their own immense gravity, presents a significant challenge to direct observation. However, astronomers have developed ingenious methods to indirectly detect and study these cosmic enigmas. The key lies in observing the effects black holes have on their surroundings – effects that are, in many cases, far more dramatic than the black holes themselves.

One of the most compelling methods is through the careful observation of the movements of stars and gas clouds orbiting a suspected black hole. If a massive, unseen object is significantly affecting the orbits of visible matter, the characteristics of that orbit can betray the presence of the unseen entity. This is particularly powerful when applied to stars orbiting close to the center of a galaxy. The speed and trajectory of these stars, measured through precise spectroscopic techniques, can reveal the presence of a supermassive black hole at the galactic core – a gravitational powerhouse holding the entire galaxy together. The orbital velocities of stars in these regions are far higher than would be expected if only the visible matter were contributing to the gravitational field. This discrepancy directly implies the presence of a far more massive, hidden object – the black hole. Years of meticulous observation and complex modeling are needed to determine not only the presence of such an object but also to estimate its mass and other properties.

This technique has been used extensively to determine the masses of supermassive black holes at the centers of numerous galaxies, including our own Milky Way. The observation of stars orbiting Sagittarius A, the radio source believed to be a supermassive black hole at the Milky Way's center, has provided compelling evidence for its existence and allowed astronomers to estimate its mass to be approximately 4 million times that of our Sun. The precision of these measurements continuously improves as observational technologies refine our ability to track stellar movements with ever-increasing accuracy. The longer the observation period, the more accurately the stellar orbits can be mapped, leading to more precise estimations of the central mass. Furthermore, the advent of highly sensitive instruments allows the detection of fainter stars, providing a larger sample size for the analysis and contributing to better statistical confidence in the mass estimation.

Another indirect method leverages the effects of black holes on accretion disks. As black holes pull in surrounding matter, this material doesn't fall straight in; instead, it forms a swirling disk of gas and dust around the black hole, known as an accretion disk. The friction within this disk heats the material to incredibly high temperatures, causing it to emit intense radiation across the electromagnetic spectrum, from radio waves to X-rays. These emissions provide a detectable signature, acting as a beacon that points to the presence of a black hole. The spectrum of this emitted radiation provides clues about the black hole's properties, including its mass, spin, and the rate at which it's accreting matter. The brighter and more energetic the radiation, the more aggressively the black hole is feeding, implying a higher accretion rate and potentially a larger black hole.

Different types of black holes display distinct accretion disk properties. Stellar-mass black holes, for instance, tend to exhibit more erratic and variable accretion, resulting in brighter and more fluctuating X-ray emissions.

Supermassive black holes, on the other hand, often display more stable accretion, resulting in a more consistent radiation output. These variations reflect the different environments in which these two types of black holes reside and the differences in the surrounding material available for accretion. Careful study of these variations helps astronomers not only detect black holes but also differentiate between stellar-mass and supermassive black holes, providing valuable insights into the formation and evolution of these celestial objects. Furthermore, the study of accretion disks allows for the analysis of the chemical composition of the material swirling into the black hole, providing clues about the environment in which the black hole resides and perhaps the history of its formation and subsequent evolution.

Beyond the electromagnetic spectrum, the detection of gravitational waves has revolutionized our ability to observe black holes. Einstein's theory of general relativity predicts that accelerating massive objects, such as merging black holes, should create ripples in the fabric of spacetime – gravitational waves. These waves, though incredibly faint, can be detected using highly sensitive interferometers, such as LIGO and Virgo. The detection of gravitational waves from merging black holes not only confirms a key prediction of Einstein's theory but also provides an entirely new window into these cosmic entities. The signals carry valuable information about the masses, spins, and distances of the merging black holes, allowing scientists to reconstruct these cosmic events and study their properties with unprecedented accuracy.

Gravitational wave astronomy allows us to study black holes in a way that is completely independent of their electromagnetic emissions. It allows observation of black holes even when they are not actively accreting material, providing a more complete picture of their population and distribution throughout the universe. Moreover, the observation of gravitational waves from merging black holes provides direct evidence of the existence of these objects and allows us to study their properties, especially the relationship between their mass and spin. This data is proving crucial in refining our theoretical models of black hole formation and evolution, as well as our understanding of the dynamics of extreme gravitational events. The frequency and amplitude of the gravitational waves detected provide direct measurements of the masses and spins of the merging black holes, information not readily accessible through electromagnetic observations.

Furthermore, the study of gravitational waves offers a unique opportunity to probe the very nature of gravity in extreme environments. The merging of black holes generates gravitational waves with frequencies that span a broad range, allowing for testing of general relativity in regimes where its predictions remain untested. Potential deviations from the predictions of general relativity would point towards the need for a more comprehensive theory of gravity, potentially a quantum theory of gravity that can unify our understanding of gravity with quantum mechanics. The quest to unravel the mysteries of black holes is intertwined with our quest to understand gravity itself.

The detection of gravitational waves is still a relatively new field, but its potential for transforming our understanding of black holes is enormous. As detectors become more sensitive and more sophisticated, we can expect to detect even fainter signals from more distant and less massive black holes, further broadening our knowledge of the black hole population and their role in the universe's evolution. The collaboration between electromagnetic observations and gravitational wave detection provides a powerful synergy, offering a multifaceted approach to unraveling the mysteries of black holes and their profound influence on the cosmos.

By combining the insights gained from these diverse methods, astronomers are building a richer and more complete picture of these enigmatic objects, continually refining our understanding of their formation, evolution, and impact on the universe. The ongoing research in this field promises even more exciting discoveries in the years to come, constantly challenging and reshaping our understanding of the universe's most extreme environments.

Black Holes and Galaxy Evolution

The profound influence of black holes extends far beyond their immediate surroundings; they play a pivotal, and often dramatic, role in the evolution of galaxies themselves. While we've discussed how astronomers detect these cosmic titans through indirect methods, their impact on galactic structure and star formation is equally compelling evidence of their existence and importance. The relationship between supermassive black holes and their host galaxies is a complex and dynamic interplay, shaping the galaxies' morphology, star formation rates, and ultimately, their destiny.

At the heart of many, if not most, galaxies resides a supermassive black hole, a behemoth millions or even billions of times more massive than our Sun. These are not simply inert objects; their immense gravitational influence orchestrates the dance of stars and gas within their galactic domains. The black hole's gravity acts as an anchor, influencing the motion of stars in the galactic core and dictating the overall distribution of matter within the galaxy. The galactic bulge, a dense region of stars often found at the center of spiral galaxies, is largely shaped by the gravitational pull of the central supermassive black hole. The density and shape of this bulge provide valuable clues about the mass and evolution of the black hole itself. Variations in the bulge's structure among different galaxies directly reflect the diverse interplay between black hole growth and galactic evolution.

Beyond the direct gravitational influence on stellar orbits, the supermassive black hole also plays a significant role in regulating star formation within the galaxy. This regulation occurs through a process known as feedback. As the black hole accretes matter from its surroundings, the friction within the accretion disk generates tremendous heat and energy, often resulting in powerful outflows of material – jets of superheated plasma that can extend far beyond the galaxy itself. These jets, propelled by the black hole's rotational energy, carry immense amounts of energy and momentum, injecting it into the interstellar medium, the gas and dust between stars.

This injection of energy can have profound consequences for star formation. The jets can disrupt the cold, dense molecular clouds that are the birthplaces of stars, preventing them from collapsing under their own gravity and forming new stars.

This disruptive process can suppress star formation in the galactic center and even across larger regions of the galaxy. The balance between the accretion rate of the black hole and the rate of star formation is a complex interplay, a carefully orchestrated dance between cosmic entities. If the black hole accretes too much matter, it can trigger powerful feedback mechanisms that effectively shut down star formation.

Conversely, a relatively quiescent black hole will exert less influence, allowing for unhindered star formation.

Observations suggest a strong correlation between the mass of the central supermassive black hole and the properties of its host galaxy, a phenomenon often referred to as the "M-σ relation." This relation shows that galaxies with more massive central black holes tend to have larger bulges, higher stellar velocity dispersions (meaning stars are moving more quickly), and in some cases, higher rates of star formation in the outer regions of the galaxy. This correlation points to a close connection between black hole growth and the overall evolution of the galaxy. Understanding this relationship is crucial in building complete models of galaxy evolution. The M-σ relation provides a constraint for these models, guiding the development of theoretical frameworks that incorporate the impact of supermassive black holes.

However, the relationship is far from simple. While the M-σ relation highlights a general trend, significant deviations are observed, suggesting additional factors influence the interplay between the black hole and its host galaxy.

Environmental factors such as mergers with other galaxies or the density of the surrounding galaxy cluster can greatly affect the growth of both the galaxy and its central black hole. For example, a galaxy that undergoes a major merger with another galaxy may experience a significant burst of star formation, accompanied by a surge in the accretion rate of its central black hole. This event dramatically alters the galaxy's morphology and star formation history, demonstrating the profound effects of galactic interactions.

The study of active galactic nuclei (AGN), galaxies with intensely bright cores powered by accreting supermassive black holes, provides further insight into this relationship. AGN are characterized by their luminous emissions across the electromagnetic spectrum, originating from the accretion disk surrounding the black hole and from relativistic jets emanating from the vicinity of the black hole. The energy output of AGN can far exceed the combined output of all the stars in their host galaxy, demonstrating the immense power of these black holes. The observation of AGN allows astronomers to directly study the processes that drive black hole growth and its effects on the surrounding galaxy.

Different types of AGN, classified based on their luminosity and spectral characteristics, reveal different aspects of black hole accretion and feedback. For instance, quasars, the most luminous AGN, are believed to be powered by exceptionally rapidly accreting supermassive black holes, their intense radiation indicating extremely high accretion rates. The observed characteristics of quasars offer crucial clues about the early universe, since these luminous AGN can be seen across vast cosmic distances. Their presence and evolution offer valuable information on the formation and growth of supermassive black holes in the early universe and the influence of these objects on the early galaxy population.

The study of AGN also reveals the feedback mechanisms mentioned earlier. Powerful jets from AGN can propagate vast distances, influencing the structure and evolution of their host galaxy and the surrounding intergalactic medium. These jets can trigger star formation in regions far from the galactic center, through compression and shocks caused by the jet interaction with the surrounding gas. This demonstrates a more complex and far-reaching influence of the black hole than simple suppression of star formation. The interplay between these various mechanisms is still under intense investigation, with advanced simulations and observational techniques continually refining our understanding of this complex relationship.

In conclusion, the relationship between supermassive black holes and galaxy evolution is a story of intricate interplay and profound influence. These cosmic vacuum cleaners, far from being mere passive inhabitants, actively shape their galactic environments, regulating star formation, influencing galactic structure, and leaving an indelible mark on the galaxies' evolutionary paths. Continued observations and theoretical modeling will undoubtedly reveal further nuances in this complex relationship, deepening our understanding of how galaxies form, evolve, and ultimately, fade away. The saga of black holes and galaxy evolution remains one of the most captivating chapters in the ongoing exploration of the cosmos, promising many further revelations as our observational capabilities and theoretical understanding continue to advance. The synergy between observational astronomy, computational astrophysics, and theoretical modelling is key to unlocking the full complexity of this intricate cosmic dance. The next generation of telescopes, both ground-based and space-based, promises to provide even more detailed information, leading us closer to a complete understanding of how these mighty entities shape the universe around them.

Black Hole Information Paradox

The journey into the heart of a black hole, while fascinating, leads us to the edge of our current understanding of physics. We've explored their immense gravitational pull and their role in shaping galaxies, but even with our advanced tools and theories, certain mysteries remain stubbornly resistant to explanation. One such enigma, a profound conceptual challenge that has captivated physicists for decades, is the black hole information paradox. This paradox delves into the very nature of information, entropy, and the laws of physics as we understand them, posing a direct challenge to the seemingly inviolable principles of quantum mechanics.

At the heart of the paradox lies the clash between general relativity, our best description of gravity and the large-scale structure of the universe, and quantum mechanics, which governs the behavior of matter at the subatomic level.

General relativity describes black holes as regions of spacetime with such intense gravity that nothing, not even light, can escape their grasp. Once matter crosses the event horizon, the boundary beyond which escape is impossible, it seems to vanish from our observable universe. This disappearance, however, creates a fundamental problem when viewed through the lens of quantum mechanics.

Quantum mechanics dictates that information cannot be truly destroyed. This principle, often referred to as unitary evolution, implies that the complete description of a quantum system, encompassing all its properties, is preserved throughout its evolution. This is fundamentally different from classical physics, where information can be lost through dissipation or irreversible processes. Think of a book burning; the information encoded within the book is, for all practical purposes, destroyed. In the quantum realm, however, the information remains, albeit potentially in a scrambled or highly complex form.

The black hole presents a seeming violation of this principle. If information falling into a black hole is lost forever, it suggests a breakdown of unitary evolution, a cornerstone of quantum mechanics. Imagine throwing a book into a black hole. The book's contents, representing a vast amount of information, would appear to be irretrievably gone. General relativity, focusing on the macroscopic behavior of gravity, doesn't address this information loss. But quantum mechanics, concerned with the fundamental building blocks of matter and their interactions, suggests it is impossible.

This discrepancy forms the essence of the black hole information paradox.

Furthermore, the problem is exacerbated by the concept of black hole evaporation, proposed by Stephen Hawking.

Hawking's groundbreaking work demonstrated that black holes are not entirely black; they emit a faint radiation, known as Hawking radiation, due to quantum effects near the event horizon. This radiation, however, is thermal in nature, meaning it carries no specific information about the matter that fell into the black hole. The information seems to be lost forever. This leads to a conflict between the fundamental principles of quantum mechanics, which demand the preservation of information, and the observed behavior of black holes as described by Hawking radiation, which seems to destroy information.

To illustrate the implications more clearly, consider a simple experiment. Let's imagine we throw a specific quantum state – perhaps a particular arrangement of particles with well- defined properties – into a black hole. According to quantum mechanics, this state should be preserved, even if its representation is complex. The information encoded in this quantum state includes all the details that define the system, from its energy and momentum to its various quantum numbers. Yet, when Hawking radiation evaporates the black hole, we only receive a chaotic, thermal output carrying little to no information about our original quantum state. The original information seems to have vanished.

Several attempts have been made to resolve this paradox. Some theories suggest that information is not actually lost but encoded in subtle ways within the Hawking radiation, perhaps in correlations between emitted particles. Others propose modifications to general relativity or quantum mechanics, perhaps a more unified theory of quantum gravity, that could reconcile these seemingly conflicting principles. The idea is that a complete theory of quantum gravity, combining our understanding of quantum mechanics and general relativity, will provide a solution. Such a theory would describe the behavior of gravity at the quantum level, near the event horizon of a black hole, where our current understanding breaks down.

One intriguing approach is the concept of "firewall" proposed by some physicists. The firewall hypothesis suggests that the event horizon of a black hole is not a smooth, continuous surface, as predicted by classical general relativity, but a highly energetic region where extreme quantum effects cause a destructive "firewall". This firewall could potentially destroy information before it crosses the event horizon, circumventing the paradox by not allowing the information to fall into the black hole in the first place.

However, this hypothesis also presents significant challenges, potentially conflicting with other well- established principles of physics.

The black hole information paradox highlights a crucial gap in our understanding of the universe. It suggests that our current frameworks of general relativity and quantum mechanics, while remarkably successful in their respective domains, are incomplete and require a deeper, more unified theory to fully describe the behavior of matter and energy under extreme gravitational conditions. The search for a solution continues to drive cutting-edge research in theoretical physics. String theory, loop quantum gravity, and other approaches all attempt to address this fundamental puzzle, striving to reconcile the conflicting aspects of general relativity and quantum mechanics.

The resolution of the black hole information paradox is expected to have far-reaching implications for our understanding of fundamental physics. It could lead to revolutionary insights into the nature of spacetime, gravity, quantum mechanics, and perhaps even the origin and fate of the universe. Finding a resolution will require a synthesis of our current understanding and the development of novel theoretical frameworks, a daunting but highly rewarding challenge. The pursuit of a solution continues to drive some of the most important work being done in fundamental physics today, pushing the boundaries of our knowledge and shaping our comprehension of the universe's deepest mysteries. It forces us to reconsider our fundamental assumptions about the nature of information and its role in the universe, challenging us to create a more complete and unified picture of reality.

The paradox also underlines the interconnectedness of seemingly disparate fields of physics. The seemingly esoteric question of information loss in black holes is intimately linked to the very foundations of quantum mechanics and our understanding of gravity. This interdisciplinary nature underscores the need for collaborative efforts, combining the expertise of physicists across various specializations. Only through such collaboration and the continual refinement of our theoretical models and observational techniques can we hope to unravel the mysteries surrounding black holes and their profound implications for our understanding of the cosmos.

The search for a solution isn't just an academic exercise; it holds the potential to transform our understanding of how the universe works at its most fundamental level. It pushes us to expand our thinking beyond the confines of our current models, fostering innovation and potentially opening doors to discoveries we can scarcely imagine. The black hole information paradox, while seemingly abstract, underscores the limitations of our current understanding and the excitement of the scientific journey still ahead. The cosmos, it seems, always has more to reveal, and the pursuit of these answers is as fundamental to the human spirit as the exploration of the stars themselves. The ongoing quest to resolve the black hole information paradox is a testament to the enduring power of human curiosity and our unwavering pursuit of a deeper understanding of the universe.

The Definition of Life and the Limits of Our Understanding

The search for extraterrestrial life, a quest that has captivated humanity for centuries, hinges on a fundamental question: what exactly *is* life? This seemingly simple query reveals itself to be surprisingly complex, a challenge that stretches the boundaries of our current scientific understanding. On Earth, we have a wealth of examples, from the microscopic bacteria thriving in hydrothermal vents to the majestic redwood trees reaching for the sky, but even with this diversity, establishing a universally applicable definition remains elusive.

One common approach focuses on identifying key characteristics shared by all known life forms. These often include the ability to reproduce, metabolize (extract energy from the environment), maintain homeostasis (internal stability), respond to stimuli, grow and develop, and adapt to changing conditions. This approach, while helpful for classifying terrestrial organisms, suffers from a critical limitation: it's based solely on our limited sample size—life as we know it. Assuming that extraterrestrial life would necessarily adhere to the same criteria is a form of anthropocentrism, a bias that could prevent us from recognizing life fundamentally different from our own.

For instance, consider metabolism. On Earth, life utilizes a remarkably consistent set of chemical reactions, largely relying on carbon-based organic molecules and liquid water as a solvent. However, could life exist without carbon? Some scientists have proposed alternative biochemistries, perhaps based on silicon or other elements. Such life might have entirely different metabolic processes, making it difficult to detect using methods tailored to carbon-based organisms. Similarly, liquid water, considered essential for life as we know it, may not be the only suitable solvent. Other liquids, such as methane or ammonia, might support different forms of life under appropriate conditions, such as those found on some of the icy moons in our solar system.

The concept of reproduction also warrants a broader perspective. On Earth, reproduction usually involves the transfer of genetic material, typically DNA or RNA, from parent to offspring. However, alternative mechanisms might exist. Imagine a self-replicating entity that doesn't rely on a linear genetic code, or one whose reproduction involves a fundamentally different process of information transfer. Our Earth-centric definitions could fail to identify such forms of life.

The challenge is amplified by the potential for extremophiles, organisms thriving in extreme environments on Earth. These organisms, like those found in deep-sea hydrothermal vents or in highly acidic environments, demonstrate remarkable adaptability and challenge our preconceived notions about life's requirements. Their existence suggests that the limits of life's capacity to survive and reproduce may be far broader than we initially imagined. If life can persist under such extreme conditions here on Earth, what possibilities exist on other planets with vastly different environments?

Furthermore, the concept of life itself might not have a single, easily defined boundary. We often think of life as a binary concept: something is either alive or it is not.

However, it's plausible that the transition from non-life to life is a gradual process, not a sharp dichotomy. Consider viruses, for example. They exhibit some characteristics of life, such as reproduction and adaptation, but lack others, such as metabolism and homeostasis. This gray area highlights the inherent difficulties in creating a universally applicable definition.

To overcome these limitations, some scientists propose a more functional definition of life, focusing on complex, self- organized systems that exhibit information processing and evolutionary adaptation. This approach shifts the focus from specific characteristics to general principles, allowing for a greater range of possibilities. Such a definition would encompass life as we know it, but it's also open to forms that differ significantly from terrestrial organisms.

However, even with a broader definition, the task of detecting extraterrestrial life remains daunting. The sheer scale of the universe and the vast distances between stars present logistical challenges. Moreover, the potential diversity of life forms means that we might need to develop a wide array of detection methods tailored to various potential forms of life. Our current search strategies often focus on detecting biosignatures – indicators of life, such as specific molecules or atmospheric compositions – but the potential variety of biosignatures could be vast and difficult to predict.

The search for extraterrestrial life is not merely an astronomical endeavor; it's deeply philosophical. The discovery of life beyond Earth would revolutionize our understanding of biology, evolution, and our place in the universe. It would challenge our assumptions about the uniqueness of life and its origins, potentially altering our perspective on the cosmos and the human race's role within it. The journey to find answers to these questions demands a constant reevaluation of our current knowledge, a recognition of the limitations of our current definitions and methodologies, and a willingness to explore uncharted territories of scientific inquiry. The quest itself, even if it remains unanswered, reflects the innate human desire to understand our place in the universe, a drive that has propelled scientific progress for centuries.

Ultimately, the definition of life and the strategies for searching for it are intertwined. As our understanding of life's diversity on Earth grows, and as we develop more sophisticated tools and techniques for detecting extraterrestrial life, our definitions will likely evolve. What seems impossible today may become a reality tomorrow. The search for life beyond Earth is a continuous exploration, a journey into the unknown that promises to transform our understanding of the universe and our place within it, forever changing the way we perceive ourselves and the cosmos we inhabit. The very act of searching, of pushing the boundaries of our knowledge and technology, is a testament to the power of human curiosity and our unwavering pursuit of understanding. It is a journey driven by the profound question: are we alone? And the answer, whatever it may be, promises to reshape our world.

Habitable Zones and the Search for Extraterrestrial Water

The search for extraterrestrial life is inextricably linked to the search for water, a molecule considered essential for life as we know it. While alternative biochemistries are possible, and we've encountered extremophiles on Earth thriving in seemingly inhospitable conditions, water's unique properties make it a prime candidate as a universal solvent for life's processes. Its polarity allows it to dissolve a wide range of substances, facilitating chemical reactions crucial for metabolism. Its high heat capacity helps regulate temperature fluctuations, providing a stable environment for biological processes. And its cohesive and adhesive properties are vital for transporting nutrients and waste products within organisms. Therefore, the identification of liquid water, either on a planet's surface or subsurface, becomes a significant indicator in the search for extraterrestrial life.

This search naturally leads us to the concept of habitable zones, also known as circumstellar habitable zones (CHZs) or Goldilocks zones. A habitable zone is the region around a star where a planet with sufficient atmospheric pressure could maintain liquid water on its surface. The precise boundaries of a habitable zone depend on several factors, primarily the star's luminosity and spectral type. More luminous stars, such as those of spectral type F, G, and K, emit more energy, pushing the habitable zone farther outward. Less luminous stars, like red dwarfs (type M), have much smaller habitable zones, closer to the star itself. The size and location of a habitable zone are also influenced by the presence of other celestial bodies that could affect a planet's climate. For example, the gravitational effects of large planets or moons can alter a planet's orbital parameters and temperature.

The concept of a habitable zone is crucial in narrowing down the search for potentially habitable exoplanets. While the detection of exoplanets themselves has become increasingly common, thanks to advancements in observational techniques like the transit method and radial velocity method, identifying those within the habitable zone is a more demanding task. It requires precise measurements of the star's properties and the planet's orbital parameters, which can be challenging even with cutting-edge technology. The habitable zone is not a static region; it can shift over time as a star's luminosity changes throughout its lifespan. For instance, a star gradually increases in luminosity as it ages, causing its habitable zone to expand outwards. This means that a planet initially within the habitable zone could eventually drift out of it, leading to the evaporation of surface water.

Moreover, the concept of the habitable zone needs to be nuanced. The simple presence of liquid water on a planet's surface doesn't automatically guarantee habitability. Other factors such as atmospheric composition, magnetic field strength, and geological activity play significant roles. A thick atmosphere can trap heat, creating a runaway greenhouse effect, rendering a planet uninhabitable despite its location within the habitable zone. Venus, for example, serves as a cautionary tale. While located within the Sun's habitable zone, its thick carbon dioxide atmosphere traps intense heat, leading to surface temperatures hot enough to melt lead. Conversely, a planet could lie within the habitable zone but lack a protective atmosphere, making it vulnerable to harmful radiation and preventing liquid water from persisting on its surface. Mars, once potentially habitable, is now a cold, dry desert due to the loss of its atmosphere.

Furthermore, the concept of surface habitability needs to be broadened to encompass subsurface environments. Icy moons, such as Europa and Enceladus in our own solar system, demonstrate the potential for subsurface oceans.

These oceans, shielded from the harsh conditions of space, might provide habitable environments for life even if the surface is frozen solid. The gravitational interactions between these moons and their host planets generate tidal forces that cause internal heating, maintaining these subsurface oceans in a liquid state. Missions like the upcoming Europa Clipper are designed to investigate these subsurface oceans for signs of life.

The search for liquid water extends beyond our solar system. Observational techniques like spectroscopy allow astronomers to analyze the atmospheric composition of exoplanets, searching for the presence of water vapor.

However, detecting liquid water directly is significantly more difficult. Future telescopes, like the Extremely Large Telescope (ELT) and the James Webb Space Telescope (JWST), will provide enhanced capabilities to study the atmospheres of exoplanets, potentially revealing the presence of liquid water. These telescopes will not only improve the sensitivity and resolution for detecting water vapor, but also enhance our ability to analyze other biosignatures associated with life. The identification of particular molecular combinations in an exoplanet's atmosphere, or even variations in atmospheric composition over time, could point towards biological activity.

The presence of water, however, is just one piece of the puzzle. The search for extraterrestrial life requires a multi- faceted approach, considering various factors beyond the simple presence of liquid water. The energy sources available for life, the availability of essential nutrients, and the planet's geological history are also crucial factors influencing habitability. Moreover, the type of life we search for depends heavily on our own biases. We tend to focus on life forms similar to those on Earth, but extraterrestrial life could differ drastically. Developing more inclusive search strategies, acknowledging the potential for radically different biochemistries and life forms, will be crucial in our quest to answer the fundamental question: are we alone?

The exploration of habitable zones and the search for extraterrestrial water are active and evolving fields of astrobiology. Advances in telescope technology, computational modeling, and our understanding of extremophiles are constantly expanding our search capabilities and refining our definitions of habitability. The ongoing exploration of our solar system and the ever- growing catalog of exoplanets promise exciting discoveries in the years to come. The discovery of life beyond Earth, whether microbial or more complex, would be a transformative event, profoundly impacting our understanding of biology, evolution, and our place in the universe. The quest is a testament to human curiosity, an ongoing journey of discovery that reveals more questions than it answers, pushing the boundaries of our knowledge and broadening our perspective on the cosmos and our place within it. The relentless pursuit of this answer is a reflection of our inherent human drive to understand our origins and our place within the grand tapestry of the universe. The journey itself, regardless of the final destination, is a profound testament to the human spirit's relentless quest for knowledge and understanding.

Biosignatures Detecting Signs of Life from Afar

The search for extraterrestrial life hinges not just on finding habitable environments, but on detecting unambiguous signs of life itself—biosignatures. These are detectable features, substances, or patterns that provide scientific evidence for past or present life. Identifying biosignatures requires a multifaceted approach, considering a range of potential indicators across various scales, from the molecular to the planetary. A single biosignature alone rarely provides definitive proof; instead, the convergence of multiple, independent lines of evidence strengthens the case for life's presence.

One of the most promising avenues for biosignature detection is the analysis of exoplanet atmospheres. Telescopes like the James Webb Space Telescope (JWST) and the upcoming Extremely Large Telescope (ELT) are capable of spectroscopic analysis, allowing astronomers to identify the chemical composition of atmospheres light-years away. Specific atmospheric gases can serve as compelling biosignatures. On Earth, the presence of oxygen (O_2) in significant quantities is a strong indicator of life, as it's constantly replenished by photosynthetic organisms.

However, oxygen can also be produced abiotically (without life), for instance through photodissociation of water molecules in the upper atmosphere. Therefore, the detection of oxygen alone isn't sufficient; it needs to be corroborated with other evidence.

Methane (CH_4) is another intriguing atmospheric constituent. On Earth, methane is primarily produced by biological processes, such as the digestion of microbes in wetlands and the raising of livestock. While there are abiotic sources of methane (volcanic activity, for instance), the presence of significant amounts of methane alongside other biosignatures could strengthen the case for life. Similarly, nitrous oxide (N2O), a byproduct of nitrogen metabolism in certain organisms, could serve as a valuable biosignature.

The detection of these gases in unusual abundance or in combinations not readily explained by abiotic processes would warrant further investigation.

Beyond specific gases, the overall atmospheric composition can reveal clues. The relative ratios of different gases, or the presence of unexpected gases, can point towards biological processes. For example, an unexpectedly high ratio of certain isotopes – variants of an element with differing numbers of neutrons – could indicate biological fractionation, a process where living organisms preferentially utilize one isotope over another. This isotopic analysis is particularly valuable because it can be more resistant to false positives caused by abiotic processes.

Atmospheric biosignatures are not limited to gases. Clouds, hazes, and aerosols can also carry information about biological activity. The presence of specific types of clouds, their distribution, and their optical properties could provide indirect evidence of life. For instance, the presence of uniquely colored clouds, or clouds with unusual optical properties, could be investigated as potentially linked to biological activity. The detection of aerosols, which are small particles suspended in the atmosphere, might also offer clues. Certain types of aerosols can be directly produced by biological processes, while others could indicate indirect effects of life on the atmosphere, such as changes in climate or weather patterns.

Moving beyond atmospheric analysis, surface features can also serve as biosignatures. The detection of large-scale biological structures, such as vast forests or algal blooms, would be undeniably suggestive of life. However, detecting such features from vast distances is incredibly challenging, even with the most advanced telescopes. More subtle surface features could be analyzed to identify indicators of past or present biological activity. For example, changes in surface reflectivity (albedo) or the detection of unusual patterns in surface temperature distribution might point towards the presence of vegetation or other biological activity.

Remote sensing techniques can help in analyzing surface features. Hyperspectral imaging, for instance, allows for the detection of subtle spectral differences in surface materials, which can be used to identify the presence of certain minerals or organic compounds that might be linked to biological processes. Radar sounding can be employed to probe the subsurface, potentially revealing information about the presence of liquid water or other subsurface features that could be suggestive of life.

Another promising avenue for biosignature detection involves the search for specific organic molecules. These are carbon-based molecules, essential for life as we know it. The detection of complex organic molecules in exoplanet atmospheres or on their surfaces would be a strong indication of life, although it would not definitively prove life's existence. Detecting these molecules require sensitive instrumentation capable of identifying very low abundances of complex organic molecules. This search includes amino acids, the building blocks of proteins, and nucleobases, the building blocks of DNA and RNA.

The challenge lies in distinguishing between abiotically produced organic molecules and those produced by life. Abiotic processes can produce simple organic molecules in space, and these molecules could be delivered to planets through comets or meteorites. However, the presence of complex organic molecules with specific chiral properties (handedness), such as the predominance of left-handed amino acids, is often considered a more robust indicator of biological processes, although this preference could also arise from other processes.

Beyond molecular biosignatures, astronomers are also exploring technosignatures – evidence of technological civilizations. These could include artificial radio signals, megastructures such as Dyson spheres, or other technologically advanced artifacts. While the search for technosignatures is currently less advanced than the search for biosignatures, it holds the potential for detecting life far beyond the limits of our current capabilities. The detection of a technosignature would not only confirm the existence of extraterrestrial life but also indicate the potential for a civilization far more advanced than our own. The search for technosignatures is inextricably linked to the Fermi Paradox – the apparent contradiction between the high probability of extraterrestrial civilizations existing and the lack of observational evidence of their existence.

Furthermore, the search for biosignatures is an evolving field, with new techniques and technologies constantly being developed. As our understanding of life's diversity and adaptability on Earth improves, our ability to interpret potential biosignatures on other planets also improves. The study of extremophiles, organisms thriving in extreme environments on Earth, helps us expand our definition of habitability and broaden our search for life beyond Earth.

These organisms demonstrate the resilience and adaptability of life, showing that life can persist in conditions previously considered inhospitable.

The search for biosignatures is a challenging but exciting endeavor. It requires interdisciplinary collaboration, combining expertise in astronomy, biology, chemistry, and planetary science. The development and deployment of new technologies, particularly in telescope design and data analysis, are essential. This journey involves refining our search strategies, improving our observational techniques, and refining our understanding of what constitutes life itself. The discovery of life beyond Earth would represent a monumental discovery, profoundly impacting our understanding of the universe and our place within it. The quest for life beyond Earth is not just a scientific endeavor; it's a human endeavor, a testament to our curiosity, our drive to explore, and our deep-seated yearning to understand our origins and our place in the cosmos. The journey itself, with its challenges and uncertainties, is an ongoing testament to the boundless human spirit of inquiry.

The Drake Equation and the Probability of Extraterrestrial Life

The search for extraterrestrial life, as we've explored, is a multifaceted endeavor encompassing the detection of biosignatures and the consideration of habitable environments. But how many such civilizations might exist? This question leads us to the Drake Equation, a thought- provoking, if somewhat controversial, framework for estimating the number of active, communicative extraterrestrial civilizations in our galaxy. Proposed by Frank Drake in 1961, the equation isn't a precise calculation but rather a heuristic tool to organize our thinking about the factors influencing the likelihood of contacting other intelligent life.

The Drake Equation is typically written as: $N = R \times fp \times ne \times fl \times fi \times fc \times L$

Where:

N represents the number of active, communicative extraterrestrial civilizations in the Milky Way galaxy. This is the ultimate quantity we're trying to estimate.

R represents the average rate of star formation in our galaxy. Astronomical observations provide reasonably good estimates for this parameter, though some uncertainty remains regarding the distribution of star formation over cosmic time. Current estimates suggest a rate of several stars forming per year.

fp represents the fraction of those stars that have planetary systems. Exoplanet discoveries in recent decades have revolutionized our understanding of planetary systems, revealing that planets are remarkably common around stars. While we're still learning about the distribution of planetary systems, current estimates place this fraction at a substantial percentage, possibly exceeding 50%. However, the types of planetary systems, their stability, and the presence of specific kinds of planets (e.g., rocky planets within the habitable zone) are all influential factors.

ne represents the average number of planets that can potentially support life per star that has planets. This is a complex factor, as it depends on the characteristics of the planets themselves, including their size, mass, composition, and atmospheric conditions. The existence of a planet within the habitable zone—the region around a star where liquid water can exist on the surface—is considered a necessary but not sufficient condition for life. Many other factors, including the presence of a stable atmosphere, a magnetic field to shield against harmful radiation, and plate tectonics, play crucial roles.

fl represents the fraction of potentially habitable planets where life actually arises. This is perhaps the most uncertain factor in the equation. While we know life arose on Earth, we don't understand the precise conditions or probabilities that led to this event. Was it a relatively common occurrence, or an exceedingly rare event? We have no comparative data from other planets to help us estimate this value.

Understanding the origins of life on Earth, involving abiogenesis, remains a major challenge. The possibility of life arising independently multiple times on a single planet is also a crucial factor.

fi represents the fraction of planets with life where intelligent life evolves. Even if life arises, it doesn't guarantee the evolution of intelligence. The evolution of intelligence is a complex process involving many factors, including environmental pressures, genetic mutations, and random chance events. On Earth, intelligence took billions of years to emerge. It is not only the time scale of evolution, but the specific environmental conditions, ecological interactions and numerous stochastic events that shape evolutionary pathways that influence the emergence of intelligence.

Whether intelligence is a common outcome of evolution or an extraordinarily rare event is currently unknown.

fc represents the fraction of civilizations that develop a technology that releases detectable signals into space. This factor accounts for the technological capabilities and societal choices of a civilization. A civilization might develop advanced technology without choosing to broadcast signals into space, or their technology might not be detectable from interstellar distances. The duration of a civilization's technological advancement and their motivation to broadcast signals are vital in determining this fraction. The possibility of a civilization's self-destruction or collapse before reaching a point of detectable technological advancement is also a pertinent factor.

L represents the length of time such civilizations release detectable signals into space. This factor is influenced by the longevity of civilizations. A civilization might exist for a relatively short period before encountering internal strife, environmental collapse, or self-destruction. Conversely, a civilization might persist for millennia, continuously broadcasting signals. Even the concept of a "civilization" itself needs careful consideration as it's a human construct that may not apply to extraterrestrial societies in ways we anticipate.

The Drake Equation's inherent uncertainty stems from our limited understanding of many of these factors. While R and fp have relatively well-constrained estimates, fl, fi, fc, and L remain highly speculative. Different scientists plug in different values based on their own assumptions, leading to vastly different estimates for N, ranging from a mere handful of civilizations to millions or even billions. Some variations on the equation incorporate additional parameters, seeking to further refine the estimation process.

The very act of creating and discussing the Drake Equation, however, has been invaluable. It compels us to grapple with fundamental questions about life, intelligence, and our place in the universe. It forces us to consider the possibility, indeed the probability, of life beyond Earth, and it encourages the development of new technologies and scientific approaches to searching for extraterrestrial life. It highlights our limited knowledge about the conditions that make life possible, highlighting the importance of continued research in astrobiology, exoplanetary science, and other related fields.

The debate surrounding the Drake Equation serves as a testament to the profound uncertainty inherent in the search for extraterrestrial life. The equation's value lies not in providing a definitive answer, but in fostering critical discussion and driving further investigation into these fundamental and ultimately, existential questions. The quest to determine the value of N is a journey of exploration, one that pushes the boundaries of scientific knowledge and challenges our deepest assumptions about our place in the cosmos. It underscores the vital importance of continued scientific inquiry and international collaboration in the pursuit of discovering whether we are alone.

The potential implications of discovering an answer, whether positive or negative, would be far-reaching, altering our understanding of biology, evolution, history, and our place within the vast expanse of the cosmos. Regardless of the final numerical answer we eventually arrive at, the journey towards understanding the possibility of extraterrestrial life continues to be one of humanity's most significant scientific endeavors. It fuels our inherent curiosity and fuels our ambition to explore the universe and seek out answers to the biggest questions humanity has ever posed. The Drake Equation, then, is not just a mathematical formula; it is a symbol of our persistent quest to understand our universe and our place within it.

The Fermi Paradox and the Great Silence

The Drake Equation, as compelling as it is, leaves us with a profound and unsettling question: if the probability of extraterrestrial civilizations is even moderately high, as some interpretations of the equation suggest, why haven't we detected any signs of them? This apparent contradiction lies at the heart of the Fermi Paradox, a thought experiment named after physicist Enrico Fermi, who famously posed the question in the 1950s. The paradox highlights the vast discrepancy between the seemingly high probability of extraterrestrial life, as suggested by the Drake Equation and our growing understanding of the prevalence of exoplanets, and the conspicuous absence of any evidence of such life.

The silence is deafening, a great cosmic silence that challenges our assumptions and fuels ongoing debate among scientists and thinkers alike.

One potential resolution to the Fermi Paradox lies in the sheer vastness of space. Even if numerous civilizations exist, the distances between stars are so immense that communication or travel between them would be an extraordinarily challenging, if not impossible, undertaking.

The distances involved translate into incredibly long travel times, even at speeds approaching the speed of light.

Consider the nearest star system, Alpha Centauri, located roughly 4.37 light-years away. This means that a radio signal sent from Earth would take over four years to reach Alpha Centauri, and any response would take another four years to return. For more distant stars, the communication delays become exponentially longer, stretching into millennia or even longer. This vastness might simply make interstellar communication and interaction practically infeasible, resulting in the silence we observe.

Another significant factor contributing to the Fermi Paradox is the potential for the relatively short lifespans of civilizations. Our own civilization's technological advancement is relatively recent, a blink of an eye in cosmic terms. If civilizations tend to collapse or self-destruct before reaching a technologically advanced state capable of interstellar communication, this could explain the absence of detectable signals. This scenario highlights the fragility of advanced civilizations and the potential for internal conflicts, environmental catastrophes, or other unforeseen events to lead to their demise. The history of civilizations on Earth provides a sobering reminder of the transient nature of complex societies. Empires rise and fall, technologies advance and become obsolete, and civilizations face numerous challenges to their continued existence. The possibility of a similar fate befalling extraterrestrial civilizations cannot be ignored.

The limitations of our detection capabilities also play a crucial role in the Fermi Paradox. Our current methods of searching for extraterrestrial life are relatively limited, focusing primarily on radio signals and other electromagnetic emissions. It's possible that other civilizations might utilize communication methods that are beyond our current detection capabilities, or that their signals are too weak or too diffused to be picked up by our instruments. Consider, for instance, the possibility of advanced civilizations employing quantum communication or other technologies that are currently beyond our comprehension. Such technologies might not produce any detectable signals using our current methods.

The possibility of different evolutionary pathways also needs consideration. It's conceivable that life and intelligence may evolve in ways that are vastly different from what we observe on Earth. Extraterrestrial civilizations might not have the same technological advancements as we do, or they might have priorities that differ greatly from our own. They might have no interest in interstellar communication, or they may have chosen to remain hidden, for reasons we can only speculate upon. The diversity of life on Earth itself hints at the potential for extraordinary variation in life forms elsewhere in the universe. This variation extends beyond simple differences in physical appearance and behavior and may also include fundamental differences in technological advancements and social structures.

Furthermore, the concept of a "civilization" itself may be anthropocentric. We assume a civilization will behave in ways that are recognizable to us, but this might be a flawed assumption. An advanced extraterrestrial civilization might have transcended our understanding of a structured society, existing in ways that are imperceptible to us. Their technological advancements might have integrated them so completely with their environment that they are essentially undetectable. Their form might be so radically different from anything we've envisioned, that our search parameters are fundamentally inadequate.

The "Zoo Hypothesis" posits that advanced civilizations are aware of our existence but have chosen not to interfere, perhaps observing us from a distance. This scenario suggests a form of cosmic quarantine, where advanced civilizations avoid contact to allow less developed civilizations to evolve naturally. This approach reflects a sense of responsibility and a recognition of the potential harm that contact might cause. The ethics of intervention in the development of other civilizations is a complex issue, and the "Zoo Hypothesis" suggests that some advanced civilizations might prioritize non-interference over direct contact.

Another intriguing hypothesis is the "Great Filter" concept. This hypothesis suggests that there is some significant hurdle or obstacle that prevents most life forms from reaching a technologically advanced state capable of interstellar communication. This filter might lie in the past, preventing life from arising in the first place, or it might lie in the future, threatening the longevity of civilizations. Identifying the location of this filter is crucial in determining our own prospects for long-term survival and the likelihood of encountering other advanced civilizations. The location of the filter, whether behind us or ahead of us, has profound implications for our understanding of the prevalence of life in the universe. If the filter lies behind us, the odds are high that we are relatively unique in the universe. If, however, the filter lies ahead of us, it suggests a future threat that could prevent our own civilization from reaching interstellar status.

The Fermi Paradox, far from being a simple question with a straightforward answer, presents a complex challenge that demands a multi-faceted approach. It forces us to confront our assumptions about the nature of life, intelligence, and civilizations. It compels us to acknowledge the limits of our current knowledge and the vast uncertainties inherent in extrapolating from a single example – life on Earth – to the universe as a whole. The ongoing debate surrounding the paradox serves as a constant reminder of the need for continued scientific exploration, pushing the boundaries of our understanding of the cosmos and our place within it. The search for extraterrestrial life is not simply a scientific endeavor; it is an exploration of our own existence and our place in the grand tapestry of the universe. The silence, therefore, may indeed be deafening, but it also serves as a powerful catalyst for further exploration and a deeper understanding of ourselves and the universe around us. The ultimate answer to the Fermi Paradox may lie beyond our current grasp, but the very pursuit of the answer fuels our scientific curiosity and drives our exploration of the cosmos. The journey itself is as important as the destination, and the questions raised by the Fermi Paradox remain fundamental to our understanding of life and the universe.

Upcoming Missions and Telescopes

The Fermi Paradox, with its unsettling silence, underscores the limitations of our current observational capabilities. Our understanding of the universe is still nascent, and our technological reach, while impressive, is dwarfed by the sheer scale of the cosmos. Fortunately, the near future holds immense promise for expanding our observational horizons, thanks to a suite of ambitious missions and powerful new telescopes. These technological advancements represent a quantum leap in our ability to search for extraterrestrial life and unravel the mysteries of the universe.

The James Webb Space Telescope (JWST), already operational, is a prime example of this technological leap. Unlike its predecessor, the Hubble Space Telescope, which primarily observed in visible and ultraviolet light, JWST is optimized for infrared observation. This capability is crucial because infrared light can penetrate dust clouds that obscure our view of the universe's early epochs and distant galaxies. By observing in the infrared, JWST can peer deeper into the cosmos, allowing us to study the formation of the earliest galaxies, observe the atmospheres of exoplanets, and potentially detect signs of life beyond our solar system. The detail and sensitivity of JWST are unprecedented, enabling astronomers to study exoplanet atmospheres with a level of precision never before possible. This precision allows them to look for biosignatures – indicators of life – such as methane, oxygen, and water vapor, in the atmospheres of potentially habitable planets. The detection of such biosignatures wouldn't guarantee the existence of life, but it would be a highly significant piece of evidence. The JWST's ability to delve into the infrared spectrum opens up a whole new realm of astronomical observation. The data already collected is revolutionising our understanding of galaxy formation, stellar evolution and planetary systems, offering glimpses into processes previously shrouded in cosmic dust. We can expect many more groundbreaking discoveries in the coming years as scientists analyze the vast amount of data JWST is generating.

Beyond JWST, a plethora of ground-based and space-based observatories are in the pipeline, promising further advancements in our ability to explore the universe. The Extremely Large Telescope (ELT), currently under construction in Chile, will be the world's largest optical/near- infrared telescope. Its massive collecting area will allow it to gather far more light than any existing telescope, enabling it to observe fainter and more distant objects with unparalleled resolution. The ELT's advanced adaptive optics systems will compensate for the blurring effects of Earth's atmosphere, providing incredibly sharp images of celestial objects. This will be crucial in the search for exoplanets and in characterizing their atmospheres. The scale of the ELT is truly impressive. Its primary mirror will be 39 meters in diameter, composed of nearly 800 individual hexagonal segments, each precisely controlled to maintain the telescope's overall shape and focusing capabilities. The sheer size and advanced technology of the ELT will significantly improve our ability to study exoplanets and their potential for habitability. The ability to detect and characterize the atmospheres of exoplanets is a crucial step in the search for extraterrestrial life. The ELT will provide a significant boost in this area.

The Square Kilometre Array (SKA), a radio telescope project spanning multiple countries, will be the largest radio telescope ever built. Its massive collecting area will allow it to detect incredibly faint radio signals from deep space, significantly enhancing our ability to search for extraterrestrial intelligence (SETI). The SKA's sensitivity and wide field of view will allow it to scan vast swathes of the sky, increasing the chances of detecting radio signals from other civilizations. The sheer scale of the SKA is a testament to the global collaboration required to tackle such an ambitious scientific endeavor. The data processing requirements of the SKA will also be enormous. Specialized supercomputers will be needed to handle the massive volume of data generated by this revolutionary instrument.

The SKA is expected to operate for decades, with continual upgrades and improvements planned along the way, ensuring it remains at the forefront of radio astronomy for many years to come.

Furthermore, future missions planned by NASA and other space agencies promise to revolutionize our understanding of the solar system and beyond. Missions to explore icy moons like Europa and Enceladus, which are believed to harbor subsurface oceans, could potentially reveal the existence of life within our own solar system. These missions will utilize advanced robotic probes equipped with sophisticated instruments to analyze the composition of these oceans and search for signs of life. These missions represent a significant step forward in the search for life beyond Earth, focusing on environments within our own solar system that might be more easily accessible than distant exoplanets.

The exploration of Mars continues to be a major focus of space exploration. Future missions are planned to return samples from Mars to Earth, allowing for more detailed analysis in advanced laboratories. The analysis of Martian samples will provide valuable insights into the planet's geological history and the potential for past or present life. The possibility of finding evidence of extinct Martian life, even microbial, would be a groundbreaking discovery.

Future missions will not just focus on sample return but also on deploying advanced rovers capable of more autonomous exploration and scientific analysis. These rovers will use more sophisticated instruments to investigate the Martian surface and sub-surface in greater detail.

The search for extraterrestrial life, therefore, is not a singular event but a continuous process of technological advancement and exploration. The forthcoming missions and telescopes represent a significant leap forward, providing us with the tools needed to answer some of the most fundamental questions about our place in the universe. The vastness of space and the challenges inherent in searching for life beyond Earth remain significant, but the relentless pursuit of knowledge and the constant development of new technologies are steadily shrinking the bounds of the unknown. The coming decades will be a pivotal era in astronomy and space exploration, with the potential to rewrite our understanding of life in the universe, forever changing our perspectives on our place within it. The success of these ambitious endeavors will depend on international collaboration, sustained investment, and the ingenuity of countless scientists and engineers.

The continued development of advanced propulsion systems also plays a crucial role in the future of space exploration.

The distances involved in interstellar travel are immense, presenting a major challenge to our current capabilities. The development of faster-than-light travel remains firmly in the realm of science fiction, but research into advanced propulsion systems, such as ion propulsion and nuclear fusion, could significantly reduce travel times to other stars. This research is crucial for making interstellar exploration a reality in the distant future. The potential benefits are enormous – not just the discovery of extraterrestrial life, but also the expansion of human civilization beyond Earth, guaranteeing its long-term survival and ensuring the continuation of human exploration. The challenges are numerous, but the potential rewards of interstellar travel are immeasurable.

Moreover, the ethical considerations associated with the discovery of extraterrestrial life are also coming into sharper focus. The potential for unexpected consequences and the need to develop responsible protocols for contact with extraterrestrial civilizations will be critically important considerations for future space missions. This requires a thoughtful and comprehensive approach, involving scientists, policymakers, and the public, to ensure that any future interaction with extraterrestrial life is conducted in a manner that is beneficial to both humanity and any extraterrestrial civilizations we might encounter. The development of a global consensus on the principles of responsible interstellar interaction will be a crucial step towards ensuring a future where such interactions are peaceful and mutually beneficial. The exploration of space is not merely a scientific endeavor; it is a journey that will inevitably raise profound ethical and philosophical questions about the nature of life and our place in the universe.

In conclusion, the future of astronomy and space exploration is bright. The upcoming missions and telescopes discussed here represent a quantum leap in our ability to explore the universe and search for life beyond Earth. The coming decades promise to be an era of unprecedented discovery, with the potential to rewrite our understanding of the cosmos and our place within it. The ongoing search for answers to the profound questions raised by the Fermi Paradox, fueled by technological advancement and unwavering human curiosity, is a testament to the enduring spirit of exploration that has driven humanity for millennia. The journey itself, with its challenges and discoveries, is as crucial as the destination, a journey that will shape not only our scientific understanding, but also our cultural and philosophical perspectives for generations to come.

Technological Advancements in Astronomy

The relentless pursuit of understanding the universe hinges critically on technological advancements. Our ability to observe, analyze, and interpret astronomical data has undergone a breathtaking transformation in recent decades, and the trajectory points towards even more dramatic progress in the years to come. This progress isn't limited to a single area; it's a multifaceted revolution encompassing telescope technology, data analysis techniques, and computational power.

One of the most significant leaps forward has been the development of adaptive optics. Traditional telescopes suffer from atmospheric blurring, which distorts the images of celestial objects. Adaptive optics systems use deformable mirrors to compensate for these distortions in real-time, producing incredibly sharp images. These systems are becoming increasingly sophisticated, capable of correcting for a wider range of atmospheric disturbances and providing even higher resolution images. This is not just an incremental improvement; it's a game-changer for fields like exoplanet research, allowing astronomers to resolve details in the atmospheres of distant planets that would otherwise be impossible to detect. The impact on our ability to study exoplanet atmospheres, to search for biosignatures, and to understand planetary formation is profound. The intricate dance of atmospheric dynamics, previously hidden behind a veil of atmospheric distortion, is now slowly becoming clear.

Beyond adaptive optics, the sheer size of telescopes continues to increase. The Extremely Large Telescope (ELT), already mentioned, is a prime example. But the trend extends beyond the ELT. We are moving towards an era of extremely large telescopes, both on the ground and in space, that will gather unprecedented amounts of light, enabling the observation of fainter, more distant objects with unparalleled detail. The design and construction of these mega-telescopes present immense engineering challenges. Precise mirror alignment, sophisticated control systems, and robust structural support are all critical considerations. The development of innovative materials, such as lightweight yet incredibly strong composites, has been instrumental in making these ambitious projects a reality. The construction of these behemoths involves a complex interplay of engineering, physics, and materials science, requiring the collaboration of experts from multiple disciplines.

The advancements in detector technology are equally crucial. Modern detectors are significantly more sensitive and efficient than their predecessors, allowing them to capture faint light signals with greater precision. This increase in sensitivity allows astronomers to observe fainter objects, to detect subtle variations in light intensity, and to capture higher-resolution spectral data. These advancements are particularly relevant in the search for exoplanets, where the faint light from a planet is often dwarfed by the light from its host star. The ability to accurately measure the subtle dimming of starlight as a planet transits its star is paramount in detecting and characterizing exoplanets. The sensitivity of modern detectors allows us to detect smaller planets, planets further from their stars, and to analyze their atmospheres with greater precision.

The exponential growth of computational power is another driving force behind progress in astronomy. Modern telescopes generate massive amounts of data, often exceeding the capacity of traditional data processing techniques. The development of advanced algorithms and high-performance computing has been essential in handling these vast datasets, allowing astronomers to extract meaningful insights from the raw data. Machine learning techniques, for example, are being increasingly used to identify patterns and anomalies in astronomical data, potentially revealing hidden structures or objects that would otherwise be missed. The use of artificial intelligence (AI) in astronomy is rapidly expanding, with applications ranging from data processing and analysis to the control of robotic telescopes. AI algorithms can sift through colossal datasets, identifying potential candidates for further investigation, and freeing up astronomers to focus on the more nuanced aspects of scientific analysis. This collaboration between human ingenuity and computational power is proving to be a potent combination.

Furthermore, the development of new observational techniques is continuously expanding our understanding of the universe. Techniques like gravitational lensing, where the gravity of massive objects bends and magnifies the light from more distant objects, allow us to observe galaxies that would otherwise be too faint to detect. Interferometry, which combines the light from multiple telescopes to achieve higher resolution than a single telescope, is another powerful technique that is constantly being refined and improved.

These sophisticated techniques require intricate coordination and precise calibration, but the rewards are enormous, allowing us to probe deeper into the cosmos than ever before.

The progress in space-based astronomy is equally dramatic. While ground-based telescopes are limited by atmospheric interference, space-based telescopes offer a clear view of the universe, free from the blurring effects of the Earth's atmosphere. The Hubble Space Telescope, despite its age, remains a remarkable instrument, and its successor, the James Webb Space Telescope, has already yielded breathtaking images and data. Future space-based observatories, planned by various space agencies, promise even greater capabilities. These observatories will be equipped with larger mirrors, more sensitive detectors, and more advanced instruments, pushing the boundaries of our observational capabilities even further. The cost and complexity of launching and maintaining space-based observatories are substantial, demanding international collaboration and substantial funding, but the scientific return is immeasurable. The continuous refinement and improvement of space-based technologies pave the path for an even deeper understanding of the cosmos.

In summary, the technological advancements in astronomy are not isolated incidents but rather a synergistic convergence of progress across multiple scientific and engineering disciplines. The improvements in telescope technology, data analysis techniques, computational power, and observational methods are pushing the boundaries of our understanding of the universe at an unprecedented pace. This ongoing technological revolution empowers us to ask and answer ever more ambitious questions about the cosmos, driving our quest to unravel the universe's deepest mysteries. The interplay between human ingenuity and technological innovation continues to shape our understanding of the universe, promising an era of extraordinary discoveries in the years to come. The journey of scientific discovery is a testament to humanity's enduring curiosity and our persistent pursuit of knowledge, a testament written in the starlight itself.

The Role of Citizen Science in Astronomy

The breathtaking advancements in observational astronomy, fueled by technological innovation, have opened up unprecedented opportunities for scientific discovery. Yet, the sheer volume of data generated by modern telescopes, coupled with the complexity of the analyses required, presents a challenge. This is where citizen science steps in, offering a powerful and increasingly vital tool to augment professional astronomical research. Citizen science projects leverage the collective efforts of volunteers—amateurs, students, and anyone with an internet connection and a penchant for discovery—to tackle tasks that would otherwise be insurmountable for professional astronomers alone.

One of the most impactful areas where citizen science shines is in data analysis. Professional astronomers, while highly skilled, simply lack the time and resources to manually sift through the terabytes, or even petabytes, of data generated by telescopes like the James Webb Space Telescope or large ground-based surveys such as the Sloan Digital Sky Survey. Citizen science projects provide a solution by breaking down these massive datasets into manageable chunks, allowing volunteers to contribute to specific tasks. For example, volunteers might be tasked with classifying galaxies based on their shape, identifying variable stars, or searching for exoplanet transit events.

The Galaxy Zoo project, a pioneering example of citizen science in astronomy, exemplifies this approach. Launched in 2007, Galaxy Zoo challenged volunteers to classify the shapes of galaxies from images taken by the Sloan Digital Sky Survey. Millions of volunteers participated, contributing to the classification of over a million galaxies. This project not only produced a comprehensive catalogue of galaxy morphologies, but also led to the discovery of new types of galaxies and unexpected patterns that were missed by algorithmic analysis alone. The success of Galaxy Zoo not only demonstrated the potential of citizen science but also spurred the creation of a multitude of similar projects focusing on various aspects of astronomy.

The power of the human eye and brain in pattern recognition remains unmatched by current algorithms, particularly when dealing with subtle or complex patterns. While AI and machine learning are rapidly advancing, they still require massive training datasets and can struggle with unexpected anomalies or edge cases. Human volunteers, on the other hand, can often spot unusual features or patterns that escape algorithmic detection, representing a critical element in the process of scientific discovery. For instance, the discovery of unusual features in galaxy morphology, the identification of previously unknown asteroids or comets from telescopic images, or the detection of subtle variations in stellar brightness that might indicate the presence of an exoplanet – all these tasks benefit significantly from the keen observational skills of citizen scientists.

Citizen science projects are not limited to image classification. They also play a vital role in data validation and verification. By independently analyzing the same data, multiple volunteers can provide a measure of redundancy and improve the accuracy and reliability of the results. This process can help to identify and eliminate errors introduced by human bias, instrument malfunction, or other factors.

This validation process is critical in ensuring the integrity of scientific findings, particularly when the datasets are massive and the stakes are high. For example, the verification of exoplanet transit signals by multiple volunteers can help to confirm the validity of the discovery and reduce the chances of false positives.

Beyond data analysis and validation, citizen science is also making valuable contributions to astronomical research through data transcription and curation. Historical astronomical archives contain a treasure trove of data, but much of it remains inaccessible due to the lack of digitalization and annotation. Citizen science projects are now actively engaging volunteers in the digitization and transcription of these historical records, making valuable data available to researchers worldwide. This process not only preserves the historical record but also allows for new scientific analyses and discoveries that were previously impossible.

Furthermore, citizen science projects are playing a critical role in public outreach and education. By engaging the public in actual scientific research, these projects foster a sense of wonder and curiosity about the universe, inspiring the next generation of scientists and engineers. The interactive nature of these projects allows participants to experience the thrill of discovery firsthand, fostering a greater appreciation for the scientific process and its importance in society. The success stories emerging from citizen science projects are also excellent tools for engaging students and promoting STEM education.

The effectiveness of citizen science in astronomy hinges on careful design and implementation. Projects must be designed with user-friendliness in mind, providing clear instructions and intuitive interfaces to ensure broad participation. Effective communication between scientists and volunteers is also crucial, ensuring that volunteers understand the scientific context of their tasks and receive timely feedback on their contributions. The successful citizen science project recognizes the volunteers as integral participants in the research process, valuing their contribution and offering a platform for feedback and interaction.

The future of citizen science in astronomy appears bright, with the potential for even more significant contributions to scientific discovery. As telescopes continue to generate ever- larger datasets, the need for human eyes and brains to analyze these data will only increase. Advances in software and data visualization techniques are making it easier than ever for volunteers to participate, and the use of sophisticated online platforms and social media tools are fostering a greater sense of community and collaboration among citizen scientists. The growth of online communities and forums focused on citizen science, where volunteers can share their knowledge, experiences, and insights, will further empower the collective efforts to unravel the mysteries of the cosmos.

Moreover, the development of more sophisticated tools for classifying and analysing astronomical data, specifically designed with citizen scientist contributions in mind, will further enhance the quality and impact of these collective efforts. This synergy between professional astronomers, software developers, and citizen scientists promises a new era of collaborative research, accelerating the pace of discovery and potentially leading to unexpected breakthroughs in our understanding of the universe. The evolution of these tools, combined with ever-improving training materials, will enable even less experienced volunteers to make meaningful contributions, broadening the reach and impact of these projects.

The integration of citizen science into the fabric of professional astronomical research is not merely a supplementary endeavor; it represents a paradigm shift. It leverages the collective intelligence and enthusiasm of a global community to tackle problems beyond the capabilities of professional researchers alone. This collaborative model, where professional scientists and amateur enthusiasts work hand-in-hand, represents a powerful and efficient approach to scientific discovery, embodying the collaborative spirit essential for tackling the vast complexities of the universe.

The continued development and integration of citizen science will undoubtedly play a significant, and possibly defining, role in the future of astronomy and our exploration of the cosmos. The stories of discoveries made by citizen scientists, often unexpected and groundbreaking, serve as a compelling testament to the power of collective endeavor and the enduring human fascination with the mysteries of space. The universe itself becomes a shared laboratory, open to exploration by all who are curious enough to participate.

Challenges and Opportunities in Space Exploration

The remarkable progress in observational astronomy, amplified by technological leaps, has undeniably expanded our horizons for scientific discovery. However, this progress also brings forth a new set of challenges, particularly in the realm of space exploration. The future of venturing beyond Earth's confines is fraught with complexities, demanding innovative solutions across technological, financial, and ethical dimensions.

One major hurdle is the sheer cost involved in space exploration. Launching even a single satellite or spacecraft can cost billions of dollars, requiring substantial investment from governments and private companies. This financial constraint often limits the scope and ambition of space missions, forcing difficult choices between competing priorities. For instance, the development of advanced propulsion systems capable of reaching distant stars remains a distant dream, largely due to the enormous financial resources that such endeavors would require. Furthermore, maintaining operational spacecraft and analyzing the immense datasets they generate also demands significant ongoing funding, demanding a sustained commitment from funding agencies. The need for international collaborations to share the financial burden and expertise becomes increasingly crucial, especially for larger-scale projects like the establishment of a permanent lunar base or a crewed mission to Mars. Such collaborations, however, bring their own complexities in terms of coordinating resources, scheduling, and aligning scientific goals.

Technological limitations also pose significant challenges. While technological advancements have been remarkable, many technological hurdles remain. For example, developing reliable and efficient propulsion systems for interstellar travel remains a major technological challenge. Chemical rockets, while well-established, are energy- inefficient for long-duration space voyages. Alternative propulsion systems, such as nuclear fusion or ion propulsion, show promise but require significant technological breakthroughs before they can be practically implemented.

The effects of prolonged space travel on the human body also present substantial challenges. Exposure to radiation, microgravity, and isolation can have deleterious effects on astronauts' physical and mental health, requiring the development of countermeasures such as advanced radiation shielding and effective strategies for maintaining crew morale and psychological well-being. Furthermore, the development of robust and reliable life support systems capable of sustaining human life during long-duration space missions is critical, demanding technological sophistication and fail-safe redundancies.

The harsh conditions of space present another significant obstacle. Extreme temperatures, radiation, and micrometeoroid impacts pose a constant threat to spacecraft and equipment. Developing materials and technologies that can withstand these harsh conditions is essential for the success of long-duration missions. This includes the development of radiation-hardened electronics, advanced thermal control systems, and protective coatings for spacecraft surfaces. The exploration of environments like the Martian surface or the Jovian moons presents even greater challenges, requiring specialized robotic systems and equipment capable of operating in extreme environments.

Autonomous robotic systems will play an increasingly critical role, capable of performing tasks in hazardous environments without direct human intervention. However, the reliability and robustness of these systems need to be significantly improved.

Beyond the technological and financial challenges, the ethical considerations of space exploration deserve careful scrutiny. The potential for contamination of other celestial bodies by Earth-based life, and the converse risk of bringing back extraterrestrial life, necessitates rigorous planetary protection protocols. Such protocols require careful planning and execution to prevent unforeseen ecological consequences. The commercialization of space also raises ethical questions about access to resources and the potential for exploitation of celestial bodies. International agreements and regulations are crucial to ensure responsible and sustainable use of space resources, preventing conflicts and promoting equitable access for all nations. Moreover, the long-term implications of space colonization on human society, including potential impacts on culture, governance, and social structures, require careful consideration. These ethical challenges require a proactive and thoughtful approach, ensuring that our exploration of space is conducted responsibly and ethically.

Despite these challenges, the opportunities presented by space exploration are immense. The potential for scientific discovery is vast, ranging from understanding the origin and evolution of the universe to searching for extraterrestrial life. Space-based telescopes offer unparalleled observational capabilities, enabling astronomers to probe the depths of the cosmos and uncover new and exciting phenomena. The exploration of other planets and moons holds the potential to revolutionize our understanding of planetary formation and evolution, as well as the potential for discovering life beyond Earth. The discovery of water ice on the Moon and Mars, for instance, suggests the possibility of utilizing these resources for human habitation and potentially fuel production for future missions.

Beyond scientific discovery, space exploration offers significant economic opportunities. The development of new technologies and materials for space applications often has spin-off benefits for other sectors, driving innovation and economic growth. The potential for resource extraction from asteroids or the Moon could provide valuable raw materials for Earth, reducing our reliance on terrestrial resources.

Furthermore, space-based industries, such as satellite communications, Earth observation, and space tourism, have the potential to generate significant economic activity. The commercialization of space is already underway, with private companies playing an increasingly important role in launching spacecraft, developing space-based infrastructure, and providing services for space exploration. The involvement of the private sector brings expertise, innovation, and financial resources that can accelerate the pace of space exploration and broaden its scope.

The future of space exploration hinges on addressing the challenges and capitalizing on the opportunities that lie ahead. This requires a concerted effort from governments, private companies, and international collaborations.

International cooperation is essential to share the costs, expertise, and risks associated with ambitious space missions. This collaboration also promotes peaceful and equitable access to space resources and ensures that space exploration is conducted responsibly. Furthermore, sustained investment in research and development is crucial for overcoming the technological hurdles that stand in the way of realizing the full potential of space exploration. Investing in the next generation of scientists and engineers is also vital to ensuring that the momentum of space exploration continues for generations to come. Educational programs designed to inspire young people to pursue careers in STEM fields, fostering a sense of wonder and curiosity about space, will be critical for building a future workforce capable of carrying the torch of space exploration forward.

Public engagement also plays a pivotal role in the future of space exploration. Fostering public interest and understanding of space exploration through educational outreach and scientific communication is essential for securing public support and ensuring the long-term sustainability of these endeavors. Public support is crucial for securing the necessary funding and political will to undertake ambitious space exploration projects. The narrative of space exploration must be presented not just as a technological and scientific endeavor, but also as a journey of human discovery, pushing the boundaries of our knowledge and inspiring future generations.

In conclusion, the future of space exploration presents a complex tapestry of challenges and opportunities.

Overcoming the technological, financial, and ethical hurdles requires a multifaceted approach, combining scientific ingenuity, international collaboration, sustained investment, and careful consideration of the ethical implications. By addressing these challenges and harnessing the potential of space exploration, humanity can unlock unprecedented scientific discoveries, drive economic growth, and inspire a new era of human adventure and discovery beyond our planet. The boundless expanse of space offers an unparalleled canvas for human ambition and ingenuity, beckoning us to explore, discover, and understand our place within the vast cosmos. The challenges are significant, but the rewards for overcoming them promise to reshape our understanding of the universe and our place within it, for generations to come.

The Search for Answers and the Pursuit of Knowledge

The pursuit of knowledge, the driving force behind astronomical exploration, is a journey characterized by both exhilarating breakthroughs and humbling setbacks. Our understanding of the cosmos is constantly evolving, shaped by the relentless questioning of established theories and the persistent search for answers to fundamental questions about our universe's origins, evolution, and ultimate fate. This insatiable curiosity, inherent to the human spirit, has propelled us from rudimentary observations of the night sky to the sophisticated technologies employed in modern astronomy. The development of increasingly powerful telescopes, both ground-based and space-based, has revolutionized our observational capabilities, enabling us to peer deeper into the universe than ever before. From the detection of exoplanets orbiting distant stars to the mapping of the cosmic microwave background radiation, each discovery unveils a new layer of complexity and wonder, prompting further investigations and expanding the boundaries of our knowledge.

The collaborative nature of scientific endeavor is paramount in this pursuit. Astronomy, in its modern form, is a truly global enterprise, transcending national borders and fostering international collaborations. The construction and operation of large-scale observatories, such as the Atacama Large Millimeter/submillimeter Array (ALMA) and the Square Kilometre Array (SKA), are prime examples of this international cooperation. These projects bring together scientists, engineers, and technicians from diverse nations, pooling their resources, expertise, and perspectives to achieve common scientific goals. The sharing of data, research findings, and technological advancements accelerates the pace of discovery and enriches our collective understanding of the universe. The open exchange of information ensures that scientific progress is not confined to individual researchers or institutions but benefits the entire global scientific community.

Beyond the realm of purely scientific collaboration, the pursuit of astronomical knowledge benefits greatly from partnerships between academic institutions, government agencies, and private companies. Government funding agencies play a crucial role in supporting fundamental research, enabling scientists to pursue ambitious projects that might not be feasible in a purely commercial environment.

Private companies, on the other hand, bring innovation and technological expertise to the table, often contributing to the development of new instruments, data analysis techniques, and space exploration technologies. This collaborative spirit fosters a symbiotic relationship, where the advancement of scientific knowledge fuels technological innovation, and vice-versa. This synergy is essential for pushing the boundaries of our capabilities in space exploration and further illuminating the mysteries of the cosmos.

The human desire to explore the cosmos is deeply ingrained in our nature, a powerful motivator that transcends purely scientific interests. This innate curiosity, this urge to unravel the universe's secrets, has driven humanity's exploration from the earliest stargazers to the ambitious space missions of today. From the Apollo missions to the ongoing exploration of Mars, our ventures into space have not only yielded scientific discoveries but have also captured the imagination of generations, inspiring countless individuals to pursue careers in science and engineering. The exploration of space is more than just a scientific pursuit; it is a testament to humanity's ambition, resilience, and unwavering belief in the power of human ingenuity.

However, the path to discovery is often fraught with challenges. The vast distances involved in space exploration present significant technological hurdles, necessitating the development of innovative propulsion systems, life support technologies, and radiation shielding techniques. The harsh conditions of space, including extreme temperatures, radiation, and micrometeoroid impacts, pose formidable challenges for spacecraft and equipment. Overcoming these obstacles requires sustained investment in research and development, fostering collaboration among scientists, engineers, and technologists from various disciplines. The development of advanced materials, sophisticated robotic systems, and AI-driven automation are crucial for achieving ambitious space exploration goals, such as the establishment of a permanent lunar base or a crewed mission to Mars.

Moreover, the ethical implications of space exploration must be carefully considered. The potential for contamination of other celestial bodies by Earth-based life, and vice versa, necessitates rigorous planetary protection protocols. The responsible use of space resources, including asteroids and planetary bodies, also requires international agreements and regulations to ensure equitable access and prevent conflicts. The long-term implications of space colonization for humanity, including cultural, social, and political consequences, require careful consideration and proactive planning. Addressing these ethical challenges is essential for ensuring the sustainability and ethical conduct of our spacefaring endeavors.

The future of astronomy and space exploration hinges on the continued pursuit of knowledge, driven by scientific curiosity and a collaborative spirit. Sustained investment in research and development, along with international cooperation, is crucial for overcoming the technological and ethical challenges that lie ahead. The inspiration of future generations to pursue careers in STEM fields, and fostering public engagement and understanding of space exploration, are vital for sustaining the momentum of human endeavor in the cosmos.

In conclusion, the ongoing quest to understand the universe is a journey of discovery that has no endpoint. The search for answers, fueled by an insatiable curiosity and a collaborative spirit, continues to reshape our understanding of the cosmos, pushing the boundaries of human knowledge and inspiring future generations to reach for the stars. Our journey into the vast expanse of space is a testament to humanity's relentless pursuit of knowledge, a testament to our unwavering belief in the power of exploration, and a testament to our profound connection to the universe itself. The future of astronomy and space exploration holds immense promise, promising not only to unveil further wonders of the cosmos but also to inspire and uplift humanity for generations to come. The challenges are immense, the rewards even greater – a future where our understanding of the universe is limited only by our ambition and ingenuity. This journey of discovery is far from over; it's only just beginning.

Acknowledgments

First and foremost, I extend my deepest gratitude to my family and friends for their unwavering support and patience throughout the writing of this book. Their encouragement and understanding were instrumental in navigating the challenges and celebrating the triumphs along the way.

Special thanks go to [Name], [Name], and [Name] for their insightful feedback and critical eye.

I am also profoundly indebted to the many scientists, researchers, and astronauts whose tireless work and groundbreaking discoveries form the foundation of this book. Their dedication to pushing the boundaries of human knowledge is truly inspiring. I am particularly grateful to [Name of specific scientist or institution] for their invaluable contributions and access to data.

My sincere appreciation also goes to the team at [Publisher's Name], particularly [Editor's Name] and [Designer's Name], for their expertise, guidance, and collaborative spirit in bringing this project to fruition. Their professionalism and commitment to excellence have been invaluable. Finally, I acknowledge the support of [Funding agency or grant name, if applicable] for their financial contribution to this endeavor.

Appendix

This appendix contains supplementary materials to complement the information presented in the main text. It includes [List brief contents, e.g., a table of key astronomical data, detailed calculations for specific examples discussed in the book, additional images or diagrams]. Specific sections within the appendix can be found by referring to the page numbers cited in the relevant chapters.

Glossary

This glossary defines key astronomical terms used throughout the book. Definitions are presented in clear, accessible language for a general audience.

Accretion Disk: A flattened, rotating disk of gas and dust orbiting a star or black hole.

Astrophysics: The branch of astronomy that employs the principles of physics and chemistry to understand the nature of celestial objects.

Black Hole: A region of spacetime with gravity so strong that nothing, not even light, can escape.

Cosmology: The study of the origin, evolution, and large- scale structure of the universe.

Exoplanet: A planet orbiting a star other than our Sun. **Galaxy:** A gravitationally bound system of stars, stellar remnants, interstellar gas, and dark matter.

Light Year: The distance light travels in one year.

Nebula: A large cloud of gas and dust in space.

Quasar: An extremely luminous and distant active galactic nucleus.

Redshift: The stretching of light waves as they travel through an expanding universe.